WINDSOR CASTLE
Official Souvenir Guide

ROYAL COLLECTION PUBLICATIONS

Published by
ROYAL COLLECTION ENTERPRISES LTD
St James's Palace, London SW1A 1JR

For a complete catalogue of current publications, please write to the
address above, or visit our website at www.royalcollection.org.uk

Text by Jonathan Marsden and Matthew Winterbottom
Picture research by Kathryn Jones and Helen Smith
© 2010 Royal Collection Enterprises Ltd
Text and reproductions of all items in the Royal Collection
© 2010 HM Queen Elizabeth II

010232 / 10

ISBN 978 1 902163 80 2

British Library Cataloguing in Publication Data:
A catalogue record of this book is available from the British Library.

Designed by Baseline Arts Ltd, Oxford
Production by Debbie Wayment
Printed and bound by Halstan Ltd, Amersham

The unique status of Windsor Castle as a working royal palace
means that paintings and works of art are sometimes moved at
short notice. Pictures and works of art are also frequently lent
from the Royal Collection to exhibitions all over the world.
The arrangement of objects and paintings may therefore
occasionally vary from that given in this book.

For ticket and booking information please contact:
Ticket Sales and Information Office
Buckingham Palace, London SW1A 1AA

Booking line: +44 (0)20 7766 7300
Group bookings: +44 (0)20 7766 7321
Fax: +44 (0)20 7930 9625
Email: bookinginfo@royalcollection.org.uk
        groupbookings@royalcollection.org.uk
        www.royalcollection.org.uk

All works reproduced are in the Royal Collection, © 2010
HM Queen Elizabeth II unless indicated otherwise below.
Royal Collection Enterprises are grateful for permission to
reproduce the following:

Front Cover Dennis Gilbert
*Pages 1, 2, 4 (top left and top right), 9 (bottom right), 11 (middle right, below
right and bottom right), 34 (middle right)* Peter Packer
Pages 4 (bottom left), 5 (bottom), 7 (bottom left), 32 (top), 43 (bottom) EMPICS
Page 5 (top) Chorley & Handford
*Pages 6 (bottom left and top right), 7 (top left), 12 (bottom left), 39 (top left),
42, 46, 53 (top), 54 (top left), 57 (all), 58 (top right), 63 (middle), 64 (right)*
Peter Smith
Pages 6 (top left), 7 (top right) Simon Roberton
Pages 10 (top), 14 (top), 80 (left) © The Dean and Canons of
St George's Chapel
Page 11 (top left) BL MS Cotton Nero 8.iv.2, fol. 2r; reproduced by
permission of the British Library
*Pages 12 (top right), 51 (top), 55 (bottom), 58 (top left), 62, 65 (bottom right),
67, 68 (top right), 70, 71 (top), 74 (right)* Mark Fiennes
Page 14 (bottom right) © The Trustees of the British Museum
Page 15 (top) MS. Ashmole 1131, fols. 168v–169r. The Bodleian
Library, University of Oxford
Page 17 (top) Palace of Westminster Collection
Page 18 (bottom) English Heritage Photographic Library and by kind
permission of Lord Braybrooke, Audley End House, Essex
Pages 28 (all), 29 (top left and right), 30 (top left), 31 (top) Royal Archives
© HM Queen Elizabeth II
Page 31 (bottom right) Illustrated London News Picture Library
Page 33 (top) Donald Insall Associates
Page 35 Angelo Hornak and by kind permission of Lord Egremont,
Petworth House, Sussex
Page 36 (top left) David Cripps
Pages 40 (top), 53 (bottom right), 77, 78, 79, 80 (right) John Freeman
Page 43 (top) The National Archives UK
Page 53 (bottom left) G. Newbery

Every effort has been made to contact copyright holders; any
omissions are inadvertent, and will be corrected in future editions
if notification of the amended credit is sent to the publisher in
writing.

Contents

GUIDE
To the
STATE APARTMENTS

Windsor Castle

WINDSOR CASTLE WAS FOUNDED by William the Conqueror (reigned 1066–87) at the end of the eleventh century. It has been the home of thirty-nine monarchs, and is the oldest royal residence in the British Isles to have remained in continuous use.

The castle is one of the official residences of Her Majesty Queen Elizabeth II. The Queen is Head of State of the United Kingdom of Great Britain and Northern Ireland, and Head of the Commonwealth. Her Majesty is also Head of State of sixteen of the Commonwealth's fifty-three member countries.

The Queen is officially in residence at Windsor twice a year, at Easter, and again in June, when the annual Garter Service is held in St George's Chapel. The castle is used as an alternative to Buckingham Palace for ceremonial visits by foreign heads of state. The Queen and The Duke of Edinburgh spend most of their private weekends at Windsor. Whenever Her Majesty is in residence, the Royal Standard, rather than the Union flag, is flown on the Round Tower.

The State Apartments are frequently used by members of the Royal Family for events in support of organisations of which they are patrons, and for the annual Windsor Festival. Royal weddings, baptisms and birthday celebrations have been held at Windsor for centuries. Most recently these have included the marriage of The Prince of Wales and The Duchess of Cornwall at Windsor Guildhall on 9 April 2005, which was followed by a Service of Prayer and Dedication in St George's Chapel and a reception in the State Apartments.

The castle is divided into three principal areas known as wards. The steeply sloping Lower Ward is the most public part of the precincts, encompassing the ecclesiastical and collegiate life of St George's Chapel and the residences of the Military Knights of Windsor. The Guard Room with its parade ground is also located in the Lower Ward, in a range of buildings against the thirteenth-century west wall.

ABOVE: *Her Majesty The Queen in Garter Robes at Windsor.*

ABOVE: *The Prince of Wales and The Duchess of Cornwall leaving St George's Chapel on their wedding day, 9 April 2005.*

RIGHT: *Aerial view of the Upper Ward from the south-east.*

ABOVE: *The Sovereign's Standard flying from the Round Tower indicates that The Queen is in residence.*

The Middle Ward is ranged around the Norman motte (mound) crowned by the Round Tower, which today accommodates the Royal Archives and Royal Photograph Collection. The residence of the Constable and Governor is at the base of the Round Tower.

The Upper Ward, reached via the so-called Norman Gate, contains the State Apartments and royal apartments arranged around the great open space of the Quadrangle, which is sometimes used as a parade ground.

RIGHT: *The Queen with the President of Poland, Lech Walesa, during his State Visit at Windsor in 1991.*

A GRAND SCALE

Windsor Castle occupies 10.5 hectares (26 acres). In the Upper Ward there are 951 rooms (including corridors and staircases), of which 225 are bedrooms.

'It is the most Romantique castle that is in the world' (SAMUEL PEPYS, *Diary*, 1666)

5

THE GUARDS AT WINDSOR

The soldiers on sentry duty within the precincts are drawn from the five regiments of Foot Guards (Coldstream, Grenadier, and Scots, Irish and Welsh Guards), of which one battalion is always stationed at Windsor. The Changing of the Guard routinely takes place at 11am on the parade ground in the Lower Ward. When the Court is in residence the ceremony takes place in the Quadrangle *(illustrated below)*.

ABOVE: *Cleaning the 500-square-metre carpet in St George's Hall.*

ABOVE: *One of the castle's electricians changing a light bulb in St George's Hall.*

Over 160 people live within the precincts, including the Constable and Governor, the Dean of Windsor and Canons of the College of St George, and the Military Knights. More than two hundred people work at the castle, among them maintenance staff, housekeepers, porters, a clockmaker, grooms and coachmen, furniture restorers, choristers, priests, policemen and soldiers, a flagman, the wardens and other staff who present the castle to the public, librarians, curators, bookbinders, conservators and archivists. These numbers increase at Easter and in June when the Court relocates to Windsor.

Within the State Apartments are displayed some of the finest works of art in the Royal Collection, many of them still in the historic settings for which they were collected or commissioned by successive monarchs, notably George IV. The Royal Collection is held by The Queen as Sovereign for her successors and the nation. The revenue from admissions to Windsor Castle is directed partly towards the maintenance of the fabric of the castle and the running of St George's Chapel, and partly to the Royal Collection Trust, a registered charity which exists to preserve the Collection and to make it as accessible as possible.

THE STATE APARTMENTS

The State Apartments have been open to the public throughout the year since 1848. During the winter period from October to March, the tour is extended to include the Semi-State Apartments *(described on pp. 66-75).* Sometimes, use of the castle by the Royal Family may cause the published opening times to be varied for short periods.

ABOVE: *Knights and Ladies of the Garter arriving for lunch with The Queen in the Waterloo Chamber on Garter Day, 2004.*

LEFT: *The Prince of Wales meeting young visitors in St George's Hall.*

Historical introduction

WINDSOR CASTLE as it appears today is the result of almost a thousand years of development, but four monarchs in particular have left their mark: William the Conqueror (r.1066–87), who founded the castle and established its outline plan and extent; Edward III (r.1327–77), who rebuilt it in a magnificent Gothic style and established the royal apartments in the Upper Ward; Charles II (r.1660–85), who transformed the medieval castle into a baroque palace; and George IV (r.1820–30), who entirely restored the exterior to conform with romantic ideals of castle architecture, and created sumptuous and richly furnished palace interiors within the ancient fabric.

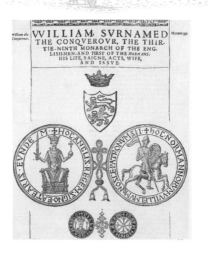

ABOVE: *An engraving of the Great Seal of William I, 'the Conqueror'.*

Norman fortress

William the Conqueror began building at Windsor around 1070, and his work was finished by 1086. The castle was built as one of a chain of fortifications around London, and occupies the only naturally defensive site in this part of the Thames valley, 30 metres (100 feet) above the river. Of the original group of castles – the others were at Berkhamsted, Hertford, Ongar, Rayleigh, Rochester, Tonbridge, Reigate and Guildford – only Windsor has survived intact. Norman castles were built to a standard plan with an artificial earth mound (motte) supporting a keep, whose entrance was protected by a fenced yard or bailey. At Windsor, unusually, there were two baileys, known today as the Upper and Lower Ward, either side of the motte. These were surrounded by a ditch which only partly survives.

The castle was built to secure the western approach to London, but easy access from the capital and proximity to a royal hunting forest (of which Windsor Great Park is the surviving portion) recommended it as a royal residence. Henry I (r.1100–1135) had domestic quarters within the castle as early as 1110, and his grandson Henry II (r.1154–89) built two sets of apartments: a state residence in the Lower Ward and a smaller lodging on the north side of the Upper Ward, which was for his family's exclusive occupation.

ABOVE: *Watercolour impression of the castle in about 1090, by Terry Ball.*

When first built, the castle was walled in timber. In the late twelfth century Henry II began to replace the outer fortifications in stone; the original Norman keep was rebuilt as the Round Tower in 1170 and over the following sixty years the entire outer perimeter was renewed. The walls were filled with the chalk found on the site, and faced with Heath stone, a durable sandy conglomerate from deposits near Bagshot, five miles to the south-west. The outer walls were punctuated with towers: those from the reign of Henry II (as on the east front) are generally square, whereas those from the reign of his grandson Henry III (r.1216–72), are D-shaped. There is a well-preserved section of Henry III's perimeter wall with its towers along Thames Street, not far from the Henry VIII Gate.

SELF-CONTAINED

The essential 'footprint' of the castle has not changed since the eleventh century. Since that time, all additional accommodation has been built within this boundary; the architectural history of the castle has involved successive encroachments on the internal open spaces.

RIGHT: *Natural pest control: 'Red', photographed here with his handler, functions as a visual deterrent to the Great Park's pigeon population, and harks back to the Park's origins as a royal hunting forest.*

9

LEFT: *Imaginary portrait of Edward III, 1615.*

BELOW: *Perspective and bird's-eye view of Windsor Castle, engraved by Wenceslaus Hollar, 1672.*

Medieval expansion

Edward III (r.1327–77), the 'warrior king' best known for his lengthy campaigns in France during the Hundred Years War, transformed Windsor from a military fortification to a Gothic palace. The massive architecture of Windsor reflects Edward III's ideal of Christian, chivalric monarchy as clearly as Louis XIV's palace at Versailles reflects French seventeenth-century ideas of centralisation and the Divine Right of Kings.

Edward III spent £50,000 on rebuilding Windsor. He began with the Lower Ward, which was transformed by new buildings for the College of St George, founded in 1352. The chapel built there by Henry III a hundred years earlier had been dedicated to St Edward the Confessor, but it was Edward III who first associated the castle and the College with St George, the patron saint of the new Order of the Garter.

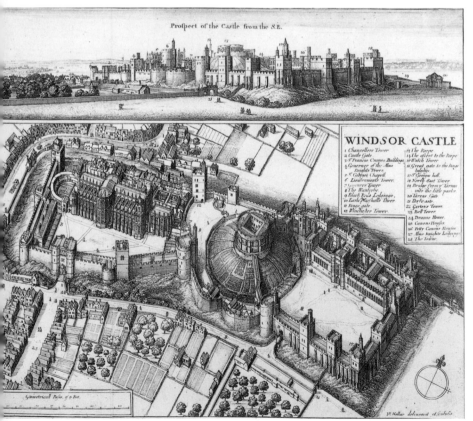

Prospect of the Castle from the S.E.

WINDSOR CASTLE

GALLETTING

Medieval masons used small chips of flint to act as spacers, ensuring that as each massive stone was lowered on to its bed of mortar it formed part of a level course. Over the centuries this technique, known as 'galletting', acquired an ornamental aspect. This purely decorative form can be found throughout the castle's external masonry, for the most part dating from the early nineteenth century.

THE ORDER OF THE GARTER

The Order of the Garter is one of the oldest and most important orders of chivalry in the world. Founded by Edward III in 1348 following his victorious return from France after the Battle of Crécy (1346) and the capture of Calais (1347), it consisted of the Sovereign, the Prince of Wales and twenty-four Knights Companion, many of whom had fought with the King in France. It is thought that the emblem of the new Order developed from a strap or band worn in battle. The motto, *Honi soit qui mal y pense* ('Shame on he who thinks evil of it'), has been interpreted as relating to Edward III's claim to the throne of France. An alternative explanation suggests that he uttered these words as he picked up a garter belonging to one of the ladies of the court, and wore it on his person.

Today the Order consists of distinguished figures in the life of the nation and Commonwealth, including former Prime Ministers. The Garter is the highest order of chivalry and remains in the gift of the Sovereign.

The military origins of the Order are embodied in the Military Knights of Windsor, retired members of the armed services who live within the Lower Ward and represent the Garter Knights at services in the chapel.

On the foundation of the Order, twenty-six 'poor knights' were appointed to pray for the Sovereign and the Knights of the Order.

The insignia, consisting of the Garter itself, the badge with St George and the dragon and the eight-pointed star with the cross of St George, can be found throughout the castle as ornamental motifs.

A three-day festival for the new Order was observed regularly at Windsor for two hundred years. Charles I (r.1625–49) placed new emphasis on the Order, adding the star badge to the insignia and reviving the annual procession at Windsor on the eve of St George's Day, but after 1674 few festivals were celebrated in their entirety.

On 23 April 1948 King George VI ordered the Knights of the Garter to assemble at Windsor to celebrate the six hundredth anniversary of the foundation of the Order, and this set the pattern for the annual 'Solemnity of St George' in mid-June, including the service and procession on Garter Day.

ABOVE LEFT: *Benjamin West (1738–1820),* Edward III and the Black Prince after the Battle of Crécy

GARTER DAY 2004:
ABOVE RIGHT: *The Queen and The Duke of Edinburgh*

RIGHT: *The Queen's Bodyguard of the Yeomen of the Guard*

BELOW RIGHT: *The Household Cavalry*

RIGHT: *The 14th-century stone-vaulted undercroft supporting St George's Hall.*

THE GOTHIC STYLE AT WINDSOR

The gothic style of building with pointed arches has remained the predominant architectural style at Windsor for eight hundred years.

Plasterwork of c.1800–1814 in the Grand Vestibule and late 20th-century gothic vaulting in the Lantern Lobby

Reconstruction of the Upper Ward began in 1357 under the direction of William of Wykeham, Bishop of Winchester. An inner gatehouse with cylindrical towers (misleadingly known as the Norman Gate) was built. On the north side of the Quadrangle, royal apartments with separate rooms for the King and his Queen, Phillipa of Hainault, were arranged around a series of internal courts. The apartments were all on the first floor, supported by stone-vaulted undercrofts that accommodated the domestic offices. These vaulted spaces, and the great kitchen to the north-east, still survive.

William of Wykeham's new buildings for Edward III took the architecture of the castle to a new level, beyond what was necessary for purely defensive purposes.

For example, the great range overlooking the Quadrangle and accommodating the King's Great Chambers, St George's Hall and the Royal Chapel was lit by seventeen tall arched windows decorated with tracery, with two matching fortified entrance towers. Safely within the precincts of the castle such defensive detailing was unnecessary, but this façade, 118 metres (389 feet) in length, was also intended to form a suitable backdrop for the magnificent tournaments staged within the Quadrangle, which acted as the castle's tilt-yard. Tournaments were one aspect of the regular gatherings of Edward III's court at Windsor known as 'hastiludes', which prefigured the court masques of the seventeenth century. Wardrobe accounts testify to the creation of the most elaborate costumes and crests, including one worn by the King in 1339 containing 3,000 peacock feathers. The helms and banners of today's Knights of the Garter in the Quire of St George's Chapel descend from these origins.

For Edward III's great rebuilding, massive quantities of stone and timber were brought to Windsor. In addition to the Heath stone used earlier for external walling, finer 'freestone' was required for the ornamental mouldings and vaults. This was brought at a rate of more than a thousand tons a year from quarries at Merstham and Reigate in Surrey, Taynton in Oxfordshire and Totternhoe in Bedfordshire; as much of the journey as possible was made by river.

Edward III's great-grandson Edward IV (r.1461–83) modernised the king and queen's great chambers and added a gallery, but essentially the late fourteenth-century apartments survived until the seventeenth century. Edward IV began the present St George's Chapel to the west of Henry III's chapel. The latter, now known as the Albert Memorial Chapel, was substantially rebuilt by Henry VII (r.1485–1509), the first Tudor monarch, who also added the range to the west of the State Apartments (on the north side of Engine Court) in 1500, probably to accommodate his own private study and library.

'...In this year [1359] the king set workmen in hand to take down much old buildings belonging to the castle of Windsor, and caused divers other fair and sumptuous works to be erected and set up in and about the same castle, so that almost all the masons and carpenters that were of any account within this land were sent for...' (HOLINSHED, *Chronicles*)

TOP: *The Garter Day feast during the reign of Charles II. This engraving by Wenceslaus Hollar shows St George's Hall as originally built for Edward III.*

BOTTOM: *The Great Kitchen, with its 14th-century timber skylight, is still in use today. Watercolour by James Stephanoff, 1817.*

Tudor Windsor

At the time of his death in 1547, Henry VIII (r.1509–47) owned sixty houses or palaces. The King travelled with his household between his many houses, which were furnished and made ready in advance of his arrival but stood empty for the rest of the year. It was at Windsor in 1522 that he received the Holy Roman Emperor Charles V for the purpose of concluding an alliance against France. Henry VIII's most significant additions to the fabric of Windsor were the gate that bears his name at the bottom of the Lower Ward, through which visitors leave the precincts, and the terrace or 'wharf' along the north side of the external walls of the Upper Ward, constructed in 1533–4. This was built of timber and supported an 'arbour' from which the King could watch the hunt in the park below. Henry also used the terrace to practise shooting at targets, while elsewhere he refurbished his father's 'tennis-play' (or court) at the foot of the motte adjacent to Engine Court.

Henry VIII was buried in St George's Chapel alongside his third and favourite wife Jane Seymour, who had died shortly

TOP: *Henry VIII with the Knights of the Garter, 1534.*

ABOVE: *Elizabeth I in the Garter procession of 1578. The new North Terrace Walk can be seen below the castle.*

RIGHT: *The royal chapel (at the end of St George's Hall) as remodelled for Elizabeth I in 1570–71. Drawing by Wenceslaus Hollar (1607–77).*

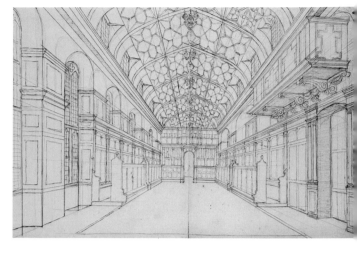

after giving birth to the future Edward VI in 1537. A grandiose monument was intended to have been set up in Henry VII's chapel incorporating a sarcophagus originally intended for Cardinal Wolsey, but although certain parts of the monument were cast in bronze it remained unfinished, and all trace was removed during the Civil War.

In 1549 the new King Edward VI (r.1547–53) complained of Windsor: 'Methinks I am in a prison; here be no galleries, nor no gardens to walk in', but his life and reign were too short to allow any improvements to the castle. His half-sister Mary I (r.1553–8) refaced many of the houses for the Military Knights in the Lower Ward, and her arms – together with those of her Spanish husband Philip II – can be found on the old belfry tower known today as Mary Tudor Tower, the residence of the Governor of the Military Knights.

By the reign of Elizabeth I (r.1558–1603), many parts of the castle were in need of repair, and an extensive campaign of work was undertaken in the 1570s. Henry VIII's terrace walk was described as 'in verie great ruyn'. Likewise the medieval royal

The Queen, it was said, 'took great Delight in being out in the Air', but hated 'to be russled by the wind'.

BELOW: *The Windsor Martyrs: Anthony Pierson, a local priest, Robert Testwood, a lay clerk of St George's, and Henry Filmer, a tailor, were condemned and burnt for heresy at Windsor in 1544. Woodcut from Foxe's Book of Martyrs.*

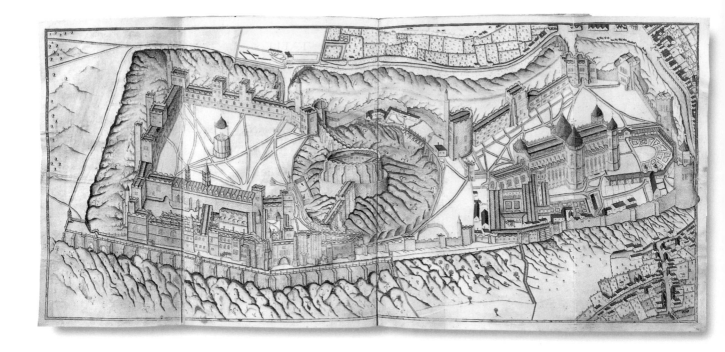

chapel, at the western end of St George's Hall overlooking the Quadrangle, was 'very ould ruinous and far oute of order redie to fale downe'.

The terrace walk was entirely renewed in stone, with an elaborate balustrade ornamented with 'ballesters, pedestalls and beastes', while the royal chapel was remodelled and refitted with stalls, a gallery and a panelled ceiling.

Overlooking the North Terrace, adjacent to the privy lodgings added by her grandfather Henry VII, Queen Elizabeth built a long gallery intended as a place to walk and admire the far prospects to the north during inclement weather. The Queen, it was said, 'took great Delight in being out in the Air', but hated 'to be russled by the wind'. Her gallery was incorporated into the Royal Library during the nineteenth century.

Windsor in the Civil War

When conflict broke out between the Crown and Parliament in 1642, Charles I raised his standard at Nottingham. Many of the royal palaces were commandeered by the Parliamentary forces, often resulting in destruction or sale, but the troops were ordered to 'take some especial care' of Windsor. Despite this,

PRINCE RUPERT

'Prince Rupert ... handsomely adorned his hall with furniture of arms, which was very singular, by so disposing the pikes, muskets, pistols, bandoleers, holsters, drums, back, breast, and head-pieces ... as to represent festoons, and that without any confusion, trophy-like'
(John Evelyn, *Diary*, 1670)

Prince Rupert's Guard Chamber in the Round Tower. Watercolour by James Stephanoff, c.1818.

LEFT: *The castle depicted in John Norden's Survey, 1607.*

RIGHT: *C.W. Cope (1811–90) The burial of Charles I at Windsor (detail), mural decoration for the Peers' Corridor of the Palace of Westminster, 1861.*

the treasury of St George's Chapel was ransacked and some of its monuments desecrated. The King's nephew, Prince Rupert, led an unsuccessful attempt to recapture the castle. This was the last time Windsor functioned as a military stronghold. The castle was frequently used by Oliver Cromwell as his headquarters, and as a prison for captured royalist officers. When the King himself returned it was as a prisoner, for his last Christmas. After his execution on 30 January 1649, his body was brought to St George's Chapel and buried in the vault occupied by the remains of Henry VIII.

Following the restoration of the monarchy in 1660, the former life of the castle was slowly resumed. The buildings of St George's were reoccupied by the clergy, and the houses in the Lower Ward rid of squatters. In 1668 Prince Rupert was appointed Constable of the castle, and instituted a new programme of repairs.

Prince Rupert of the Rhine (1619–82). Engraving after William Dobson, c.1646.

17

ABOVE: *Charles II by Antonio Verrio. Fragment of the painted plaster ceiling of St George's Hall, c.1683*

BELOW: *Peter Lely, Self-portrait with Hugh May, c.1675. The architect holds a plan of the castle, which also appears in the background.*

Charles II and the 'English Versailles'

Charles II was determined to reinstate Windsor as his principal non-metropolitan palace. It was his father's burial-place, and his restoration of the castle, and of the full ceremonial of the Garter, were important symbols of the restoration of the monarchy itself. The gentleman-architect Hugh May (1621–84), who had been with the King in exile in Holland, was appointed in 1673 to supervise the modernisation of the royal apartments, which were to become the grandest baroque State Apartments in England. The work took eleven years to complete.

Hugh May's work entailed very extensive refenestration. The ancient defensive walls were now pierced by tall, round-headed windows, and on the north side the ancient line of the castle wall was broken through to form the principal royal lodgings. This new range was known as the Star Building, from the giant carved and painted Garter Star applied to the façade. The new apartments created for the King and his Queen, Catherine of Braganza, followed the sequence that had evolved over several

'... Wee have thought fit to pull downe and alter in severall places the outwalls and other the buildings in Our Royal Castle of Windsor, for making Our apartment and Lodgings the more convenient.'

(KING CHARLES II, *Warrant dated 27 September 1675*)

RIGHT: *J.M. Wright,* Charles II in Parliament robes, *c.1670*

hundred years and occupied much the same spaces as former monarchs had used, but the architecture and decoration were now dictated by the strict protocol of the restored court. Each set of apartments began with a guard chamber bristling with weaponry, reminding the visitor that the royal persons were well guarded. There followed in succession the presence chamber, privy chamber, withdrawing room, great and little bedchambers, and closet. The King conducted most of his important business in the withdrawing room, great chamber and private rooms beyond, and access was strictly regulated.

May assembled a formidable team of artists and craftsmen to work throughout the new apartments. The Neapolitan mural painter Antonio Verrio (*c.*1640–1721) was appointed 'Servant in Ordinary to his Majesty imployed in Paynting and adorning His Majesty's building in Windsor Castle'. He painted twenty-three ceilings, and the walls of the staircases to the King and Queen's apartments, with mythological scenes glorifying the restored dynasty; whilst in St George's Hall the whole 33.5-metre (110-foot) north wall was devoted to a victory procession for the Black Prince, greeted by his father Edward III. The new St George's Hall was paved in black and white marble, and at its eastern end a broad, stepped dais supported an elaborately carved and gilded throne of state, surrounded by figures of Fame, Justice and Prudence. In the chapel at the other end of the Hall, Verrio depicted Christ's acts of healing.

These murals were accompanied by virtuoso compositions in carved limewood by Grinling Gibbons (1648–1721) and his assistant Henry Phillips, while the gilder René Cousin added embellishments and illusionistic touches such as *trompe-l'œil* sculptures on the King's staircase. The richness of the apartments was everywhere heightened by expensive textiles: fringed velvets with gold and silver embroidery for the throne canopies and beds, and magnificent tapestries. To preserve their colours, these were exposed only when the King and Queen were in residence. The rooms were filled with works of art formerly in the collection of Charles I, sold under Cromwell

'The King brought in a politer way of living which passed to luxury and intolerable expense'
(JOHN EVELYN, *Diary*)

LEFT: *The chapel designed by May, with murals by Verrio and carvings by Grinling Gibbons. Watercolour by Charles Wild,* c.1818.

OPPOSITE: *St George's Hall with decorations by Verrio and Gibbons. Watercolour by Charles Wild,* c.1818.

ABOVE: *Peter Lely,* Barbara Villiers, Duchess of Cleveland, *c.1665. One of Charles II's mistresses, she bore him at least six children.*

but subsequently recovered, such as the colossal portraits of the late King and his family by Van Dyck. Further works were newly acquired by or presented to the King.

Charles II loved Windsor, particularly in late summer and autumn, when there would be hunting, and horseracing at Datchet. In 1674 he staged a re-creation of the siege of Maastricht (which had taken place in the previous year) on the meadows between the castle and the river, watched from the North Terrace by an audience of a thousand.

In his transformation of Windsor, completed in 1683, the King was conscious of the shining example of his first cousin Louis XIV, who since his majority in 1661 had undertaken an unprecedented campaign of building and artistic patronage, above all at Versailles and the Louvre, using architectural magnificence both as an instrument of diplomacy and as a demonstration of the permanence of his right to rule. The Long Walk, an avenue of elm trees stretching two and a half miles south of the castle, was planted from 1680 in much the same spirit (it was replanted in 1945). Charles II emulated his French cousin in other ways: there was a playhouse within the castle, with a troupe of 'French comoedians', and music was provided by a new court orchestra known as the Twenty Four Violins, based directly on that of Louis XIV.

Charles II's apartments survived virtually unchanged to the end of the eighteenth century. Among his immediate successors, William III (r.1689–1702) concentrated his attentions on the Tudor palace of Hampton Court, which was vastly extended by Sir Christopher Wren, and on Kensington Palace, created from a house purchased from the Earl of Nottingham.

Wren, whose father was Dean of Windsor, had been appointed Comptroller of the Works at Windsor on the death of Hugh May in 1684. He produced a grand design for the rebuilding of the south range of the Upper Ward, but this remained unexecuted at the time of William III's death in 1702. The same was true of the mausoleum dedicated to the memory of Charles I, which he proposed for the site of the Henry VII Chapel. Wren also supplied William and Mary with designs for extensive formal gardens on all sides of the castle (as did the ageing French royal gardener of Versailles, André Le Nôtre), but these were also left unrealised in the King's lifetime. Wren's only significant work at Windsor was the completion of the town Court House (now Guildhall) in 1688, following the death of its designer Sir Thomas Fitch.

Queen Anne (r.1702–14), the daughter of James II, was born at Windsor and retained a special affection for the castle. She purchased and enlarged a small eighteenth-century house known as the Queen's Garden House on the south side. On coming to the throne she took to using her uncle Charles II's modern State Apartments, but the Garden House remained her favourite Windsor residence. She put in hand the laying out of a spectacular parterre on the north side of the castle, known as the Maastricht Garden after the mock battle staged there by Charles II. The garden stretched from the north slopes of the castle as far as the river, but was abandoned to meadow soon after her death.

RIGHT: *Godfrey Kneller,* Queen Anne, *c.1702–4*

'The Canopy was so rich and Curled up and in some places so Full it Looked very Glorious, and was newly made to give audience to the French Embassadour to show ye Grandeur and magnificence of the British Monarch – some of these Foolerys are requisite sometymes to Create admiration and regard to keep up the state of a Kingdom and nation.'

(CELIA FIENNES, *Diary*, 1702)

George III: the return to Windsor

The early Hanoverian monarchs followed William and Mary in favouring Hampton Court and Kensington, in conjunction with the palaces of their German electorate, and it was not until the reign of George III (r. 1760–1820) that Windsor became once again an important centre of court life. For the first twenty years of his reign George III made few changes except for a vast extension to Queen Anne's Garden House, which took on a somewhat barrack-like appearance and became known as the Queen's Lodge. Partly designed by the King himself, it was the Windsor residence of the King and Queen and their growing family.

ABOVE: South-east view of Windsor Castle, *engraving, 1783. The Queen's Lodge is the long building in the centre.*

BELOW: View of the Quadrangle, *watercolour by Paul Sandby, 1770s.*

George III was the first Hanoverian born and educated in Britain, and in his study of English history he absorbed the values of chivalry promoted at the time by scholars such as Richard Hurd, Bishop of Worcester. Hurd (subsequently appointed tutor to George III's sons) probably inspired the King in the 1780s to commission for Windsor from Benjamin West an ambitious cycle of large-scale paintings of the life of Edward III and the Black Prince, in succession to those painted by Verrio for Charles II.

WINDSOR UNIFORM

George III devised a special Windsor uniform comprising full dress and undress coats in navy blue with red facings. The uniform is worn at Windsor by members of the Royal Family today, and is reflected in the uniform worn by the wardens on duty when the castle is open.

RIGHT: His Majesty King George III returning from hunting, *aquatint, 1820.*
The King and his sons are wearing the Windsor uniform.

ABOVE: View of the inside of the Henry VIII Gate, *watercolour by Paul Sandby, 1770s.*

BELOW: *Frogmore House, less than a mile from the castle. The estate was acquired by Queen Charlotte in 1792 as a private retreat.*

From 1781, when a set of apartments within the east range of the Upper Ward was refurbished for the use of George, Prince of Wales, the royal family gradually began to reoccupy the castle; new rooms in the same area were provided for Queen Charlotte in the 1790s and several of the baroque State Apartments on the north side of the Quadrangle were given a neoclassical dressing. An emphatic change in tempo and style followed the appointment in 1796 of James Wyatt (1746–1813) as Surveyor-General of the Office of Works. Wyatt's facility in the gothic style enabled George III to embark from 1803 on a restoration of the external façades and the creation of a new grand staircase to the State Apartments, whose plaster ceiling and lantern survive in the Grand Vestibule today. Once again at a time of national crisis with the menace of republican France, Windsor was recognised as a symbolic bastion of monarchy and the nation. The re-gothicisation of the castle and renewed emphasis on chivalry and the Order of the Garter may be seen as the King's response to the new threat.

Wyatt was employed to extend and refurbish Frogmore House, south of the castle, as a retreat for Queen Charlotte; here she built up a substantial library and collection of decorative art, assisted by her daughters.

Frogmore House was extensively restored during the 1980s and early 1990s, and is still used regularly by the Royal Family. It is open to the public on certain days in May and August.

George IV: a palace within a castle

When George IV succeeded to the throne in 1820, he determined to continue the gothic transformation of the castle, combined with the creation of comfortable and palatial royal apartments. He was strongly influenced by his artistic adviser, Sir Charles Long, later Lord Farnborough. In 1823 Long drew up an informal brief for a competition for the work. Mindful as George III had been of the symbolic importance of Windsor, George IV and Long intended that the exterior, perforated by Charles II's Star Building with its rows of tall windows, should once more be given an imposing, castle-like appearance. This would entail the heightening of Henry II's Round Tower, the reclothing of the exterior in massive masonry and the addition of towers and battlements. In the Upper Ward, long-standing problems of circulation between sets of private apartments on the south and east sides would be overcome by adding a 168-metre (550-foot) gallery, the so-called Grand Corridor, built in the Perpendicular gothic style against the existing walls on the Quadrangle side. The State Apartments on the north side would be given a new grand entrance and staircase, and two colossal new spaces: the Waterloo Chamber celebrating the defeat of Napoleon Bonaparte in 1815, and an extended St George's Hall, taking in the space occupied by the royal chapel.

Leading architects were asked to submit plans, and the late James Wyatt's nephew Jeffry Wyatt was awarded the task. He carried out Long's programme to the last detail, creating the present appearance of the Upper Ward; he earned a knighthood and the King's permission to gothicise his own surname, which he changed to the more Norman-sounding Wyatville. Inside the castle, a new suite of rooms facing east was fitted up in the grandest manner, partly incorporating fixtures such as chimneypieces and panelling from Carlton House, the King's former London residence, dismantled after he ascended the throne. The firm of Morel & Seddon was awarded a contract amounting to £270,000 to supply modern furnishings – seat furniture, bedroom suites and upholstery, much of it in the latest French Empire style. Morel & Seddon's draughtsmen (including the young A.W.N. Pugin and his father Augustus) prepared exquisite 'miniature designs' for the decoration of the rooms and the incorporation of works of art from Carlton House. In addition, George IV and Long embarked on a

ABOVE: *Sir Thomas Lawrence,* George IV, *c.1820*

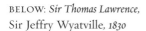

BELOW: *Sir Thomas Lawrence,* Sir Jeffry Wyatville, *1830*

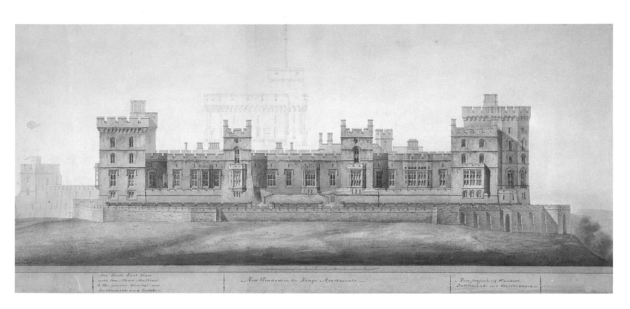

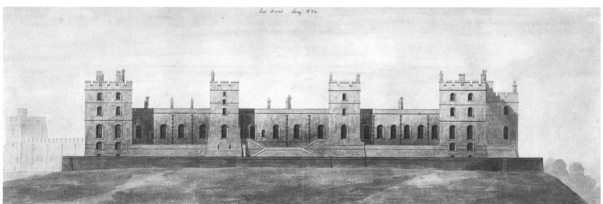

Watercolour design by Sir Jeffry Wyatville for the East Front of the castle (above), and a view of the existing front, 1824.

determined campaign to acquire antique furniture, tapestries and bronzes in salerooms and through agents in France. At the London sale of the collection of George Watson Taylor in 1825 the King purchased thirty-one lots, including masterpieces of eighteenth-century French royal cabinet-making by Jean-Henri Riesener, marble busts by Coysevox and bronzes by Leone Leoni, while Long procured thirty-eight French eighteenth-century tapestries from Paris. The displays of arms in St George's Hall, on the Grand Staircase and in the Queen's Guard Chamber were newly arranged by the antiquary and collector Sir Samuel Rush Meyrick.

George IV took up residence in the castle in 1828. His improvements, which would eventually cost nearly £300,000, were widely praised. Lady Dover wrote on seeing the Grand Corridor in January 1829 that it was 'the most strikingly

George IV and Long embarked on a determined campaign to acquire antique furniture, tapestries and bronzes in salerooms and through agents in France.

beautiful thing you can conceive', while Lady Georgiana Ellis found the extensive use of gold leaf contributed a 'fairy-like appearance' to the new apartments. The King had only eighteen months to enjoy his new castle. He died at the age of 67 in June 1830. The refurbishment of the old State Apartments continued under Wyatville's direction, but on a reduced budget.

George IV's work extended to the gardens surrounding the castle, where on the east front he laid out a D-shaped parterre of beds bordered by raised walks and punctuated by numerous marble and bronze statues and vases, brought to Windsor from several of the older palaces including Hampton Court.

ABOVE: The East Terrace garden, *lithograph by Joseph Nash, 1848 (detail)*

BELOW: *Watercolour design for the Large Drawing Room (Crimson Drawing Room) by Morel & Seddon, c.1826*

Victorian heyday

In many ways the castle enjoyed a golden age during the long reign of Queen Victoria (r.1837–1901). It served both as a rural retreat from London and a magnificent palace in which to entertain foreign heads of state, while the Home Park and Great Park provided a setting for some of Prince Albert's interests. He designed model farms and a dairy, and a vast kitchen garden capable of providing fresh fruit, vegetables and flowers for the castle at all times of year. King Louis-Philippe of France and Tsar Nicholas I of Russia were entertained in state at Windsor in 1844, as were the Emperor Napoleon III in 1855 and a succession of other crowned heads and dignitaries. The castle became the focus for the expanding British Empire and for much of royal Europe, many of whose families were related to the Queen.

ABOVE: Queen Victoria and Louis-Philippe of France driving out from the Quadrangle, 10 October 1844, *watercolour by Joseph Nash. The charabanc was a gift of the French monarch and survives in the Royal Mews at Buckingham Palace.*

RIGHT: *Sir Edwin Landseer,* Windsor Castle in modern times, *1840–43*

Queen Victoria spent the greatest portion of each year at Windsor, which became the setting for family gatherings and entertainments in addition to state occasions. The weddings of her eldest children – the Princess Royal to the Crown Prince of Prussia in 1858, and the Prince of Wales to Princess Alexandra of Denmark in 1863 - were both celebrated there. Visiting celebrities, from Franz Liszt to Buffalo Bill, came and performed for the royal family. Certain guests would be invited to 'dine and sleep' at the castle, a tradition that continues today over the Easter season and around the time of the Garter ceremony each June.

Queen Victoria decided that the State Apartments should be opened regularly to the public from 1848; during the second half of the century around sixty thousand visitors passed through the rooms each year. From 1842 Brunel's Great Western Railway brought Windsor within range for a day-trip from London, and the Queen herself began to use the train for her journeys to and from the capital. Throughout the twenty years of their married life the royal couple received at Windsor the numerous artists and sculptors who created their best-known likenesses, such as the painters Edwin Landseer and Franz Xaver Winterhalter, and the sculptors Carlo Marochetti and Joseph Edgar Boehm. Prince Albert reorganised the Royal Library and created the Print Room at the north-western end of the State Apartments, classifying and re-ordering its rich holdings and assembling a remarkable collection of reproductions of the works of Raphael.

MUSIC AND PERFORMANCE

Throughout Queen Victoria's reign the castle was used for musical and theatrical entertainments. Schubert's 'Great' C major symphony was performed for the first time in England by the Queen's private band during a concert in the Waterloo Chamber. Many composers and soloists played in private for Queen Victoria at Windsor, including Ignace Paderewski in 1891, and Franz Liszt and Edvard Grieg in 1897. Throughout the 1850s, theatrical seasons were held in the King's Drawing Room, with productions of Shakespeare and contemporary plays masterminded by the actor-manager Charles Kean.
Such performances have remained a Windsor tradition (*see page 43*).

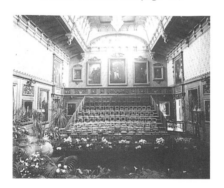

A performance of Bizet's Carmen *in the Waterloo Chamber in 1892.*

LEFT: *Menu for Christmas dinner at Windsor, 1899.*

FAR LEFT: *Victoria, Princess Royal, and Crown Prince Frederick of Prussia at the time of their marriage at Windsor, 1858.*

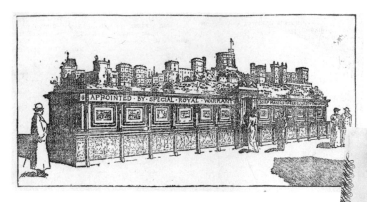

LEFT: *Scale model of Windsor Castle made of soap by Lever Bros., exhibited at the World's Fair in Chicago, 1893.*

BELOW: *Admission ticket dated 1848, the first year of the opening of the State Apartments.*

Following George IV's comprehensive restoration, very little needed to be done to the castle during Queen Victoria's reign, but some essentials remained to be completed. The royal mews and riding school south of the castle, though first designed by Wyatville and begun under William IV, were only carried to completion in the 1840s by Wyatville's former assistant Henry Ashton. Within the State Apartments, a new private chapel, designed by Edward Blore, was created at the eastern end of St George's Hall, and modern heating and fire precautions were introduced. In 1867 Wyatville's grand staircase was replaced by another rising in a different direction, designed by Anthony Salvin. Salvin's most visible contribution to the castle was the steep, curving slate roof to the Curfew Tower at the north-western corner of the Lower Ward, inspired by the work of Viollet-le-Duc at Carcassonne in France.

After Prince Albert's premature death in 1861 Queen Victoria employed the architect A.J. Humbert and her husband's chief artistic adviser Ludwig Grüner to construct a richly ornamented mausoleum in the grounds of Frogmore House in the Home Park. Here she would join her husband forty years later. As a more public memorial, the Queen renamed Henry VII's chapel in the Lower Ward, where an effigy of the Prince was installed.

Design by Ludwig Grüner for the interior of the Royal Mausoleum at Frogmore, 1863.

LEFT: *Members of the Windsor Castle Salvage Corps, founded in 1905.*

RIGHT: *Simon Elwes,* Queen Mary, 1933–4

BELOW: *Sir Oswald Birley,* King George V, 1934. *The King wears the Windsor uniform and stands beside the silver table made for William III (now in the Queen's Ballroom).*

The House of Windsor

King Edward VII (r.1901–10) reacted against the rather sombre and increasingly cluttered character that the interior of the castle had acquired during the latter part of Queen Victoria's reign. The Grand Vestibule and Queen's Guard Chamber in particular had filled up with innumerable gifts brought by state visitors or sent at the time of the Golden and Diamond Jubilees in 1887 and 1897. The new King simplified and rearranged the contents of many of these and other rooms, and he modernised the private apartments, extending the use of electric lighting and introducing central heating and bathrooms. The Surveyor of The King's Works of Art, Guy Laking, redisplayed the armour and trophies on the Grand Staircase, in the Guard Chamber and St George's Hall, and the principal State Apartments were rehung with silk damask and the pictures cleaned.

King George V, the first monarch of the new House of Windsor (r.1910–36), continued this work with his consort Queen Mary. In the energy she devoted to the preservation of Windsor and its collections Queen Mary was driven by a pride in her family's history and a real understanding of the symbolic importance of the castle in dangerous times. The First World War brought two of Queen Victoria's grandchildren, King George V and Kaiser Wilhelm II, into direct conflict.

LEFT: *Anti-aircraft defences on the East Terrace during the First World War.*

BELOW LEFT: *John Piper,* The Round Tower from the roof of St George's Chapel, *c.1942–9*

BELOW RIGHT: *The Princesses Elizabeth and Margaret Rose during the rehearsal of a wartime pantomime at Windsor.*

The First World War brought two of Queen Victoria's grandchildren, King George V and Kaiser Wilhelm II, into direct conflict.

Following the renewed outbreak of war in Europe in 1939, Queen Mary's daughter-in-law Queen Elizabeth, consort of King George VI, commissioned a remarkable series of views of Windsor from John Piper, inspired by those made in the time of George III by Paul Sandby and a contribution to the recording of national monuments in the face of the threat from the air. At the height of the bombardments in 1940, while the King and Queen resolutely remained at Buckingham Palace, the Princesses Elizabeth and Margaret (then aged 14 and 9) lived at Windsor, where their parents joined them each weekend. Each Christmas a pantomime was performed in the Waterloo Chamber, where temporary murals were fitted to the frames vacated by Lawrence's great series of portraits, which had been removed for safety.

The fire of 1992

The wartime bombing raids left Windsor remarkably unscathed. Fifty years later, on 20 November 1992, a far greater catastrophe came in the form of the fire which broke out in Queen Victoria's private chapel. It is thought to have been caused by a spotlight igniting a curtain above the altar. The fire spread rapidly through the roofspaces, destroying the ceilings of St George's Hall and the Grand Reception Room, as well as gutting the private chapel, State Dining Room, Crimson Drawing Room and dozens of ancillary rooms on adjacent floors. After a fifteen-hour struggle by two hundred firefighters from seven brigades, the fire's spread was restricted to the north-eastern corner of the castle. Despite this, thousands of works of art from the Upper Ward, including much of the contents of the Library and Print Room, had to be evacuated and put in storage. By a stroke of good fortune, the fire only affected areas previously emptied of their contents to allow the renewal of electrical wiring and other services. The survival of so many great works of art which had either been acquired or commissioned for the damaged rooms was an important consideration in the debate about their reconstruction.

Repair and restoration began immediately after the fire. The most urgent tasks were to protect the exposed building from the elements and to dry it out: one and a half million gallons of water had been pumped into the ancient masonry and timbers. The Restoration Committee, chaired by The Duke of Edinburgh, oversaw the project as a whole, while The Prince of Wales presided over the Art and Design Committee. Generally, those areas that had been most badly damaged – such as St George's Hall – were redesigned in a modern gothic style by Giles Downes of the Sidell Gibson partnership, while the other areas were restored by Donald Insall & Associates to the condition in which they had been left by Wyatville and George IV. The work was completed six months early on 20 November 1997, the Golden Wedding Anniversary of The Queen and The Duke of Edinburgh, and exactly five years after the outbreak of the fire. The cost, £37 million, was largely met from the proceeds of admissions to the castle precincts and to Buckingham Palace, which was opened to the public for the first time in 1993, supplemented by funds from the existing Parliamentary grant for the maintenance of the castle.

LEFT: *The Brunswick Tower outlined against the fire in the Upper Ward.*

BELOW: *Gilding the new ceiling of the Grand Reception Room, 1997.*

The reconstruction process brought many benefits. Much more is known about the early history of the castle as the result of extensive archaeological work by English Heritage, and although the task of maintenance is never ending, the castle is now in better condition than at any time for the last two hundred years.

The most recent addition to the castle is the garden laid out on Castle Hill in 2002 to mark The Queen's Golden Jubilee. Designed by Tom Stuart-Smith, the garden incorporates a bandstand where musicians of the Household Division play at certain times during the summer months.

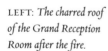

LEFT: *The charred roof of the Grand Reception Room after the fire.*

RIGHT: *The Golden Jubilee garden on Castle Hill, completed in 2002.*

Tour of the Castle

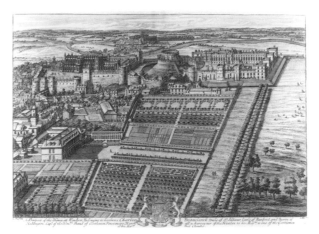

Castle Hill

The modern visitor approaches the castle along the line of an ancient road towards Datchet to the east, which skirted the curtain wall and passed through the Home Park. The road was lined with houses and working yards, including those dedicated to maintaining the castle. The area was landscaped as part of George IV's comprehensive improvements in the 1820s, and more recently in 2002 for The Queen's Golden Jubilee.

Middle Ward

The Middle Ward was originally the space contained within a wall that skirted the motte and Round Tower. This wall was associated with a ditch, of which the sunken yard in front of the Deanery is the last vestige. The ditch could be crossed by means of bridges at the Rubbish Gate (approximately where the visitor enters today) and a more imposing gatehouse between the present Middle Ward Shop and the Henry III Tower.

Since the eighteenth century the moat surrounding the Round Tower has been maintained as an ornamental garden attached to the residence of the Constable and Governor.

TOP: *View of the 'Elizabethan' gate on Castle Hill, watercolour by Paul Sandby, c.1765.*

ABOVE: *Aerial view of the castle from the south, engraving by Johannes Kip, 1707.*

ABOVE RIGHT: *The moat garden and the Norman Gate.*

North Terrace

The splendid view from the North Terrace across the Thames towards Eton was described by Samuel Pepys as 'the best in the World'. A timber walkway was first built on this site by Henry VIII. During the 1570s Elizabeth I replaced it with a stone terrace.

The North Terrace was adapted as part of Charles II's restoration of the castle in the 1670s, to accommodate his new

ABOVE: *Jan Griffier*, Windsor Castle from the north, with Eton College, *c.1680s*

Star Building (see p. 18). During the eighteenth and early nineteenth centuries daily promenades took place on the terraces around the castle and the royal family took part whenever they were in residence. A band played on the East Terrace every day except Tuesdays and Saturdays. On Sundays the castle residents and local townsfolk were joined by crowds from the surrounding countryside and London.

The prominent domed white stucco building in the distance is Stoke Park, which was designed by James Wyatt for John Penn, grandson of the founder of Pennsylvania.

The North Terrace was extended by Wyatville in the 1820s along the northern edge of the East Terrace Garden, to provide magnificent views of the east front. The sundial on the terrace was made by Henry Wynne in 1677–8 and stands on a pedestal carved by Grinling Gibbons.

ETON COLLEGE

The North Terrace affords an excellent view of Eton College with its chapel which, like St George's, is one of the great glories of English Perpendicular Gothic architecture, completed in 1482. The college was established by Henry VI with 25 scholars in 1440. Today some 1,300 boys between the ages of 13 and 18 study there.

Queen Mary's Dolls' House

This famous dolls' house, built for Queen Mary in 1924, was never intended as a child's plaything. It was initiated by King George V's cousin Princess Marie Louise (1872–1956) and her great friend the architect Sir Edwin Lutyens (1869–1944). Lutyens intended to make an accurate record of an aristocratic London house of the time. The house has running water and electricity, and is filled with thousands of objects made by leading artists, designers and craftsmen, nearly all on the tiny scale of one to twelve. The house has been described as 'a monument in minute perfection of all that was best in British workmanship.' The garden was designed by Gertrude Jekyll (1843–1932) and is ingeniously housed in the basement drawer.

The finished house was shown at the British Empire Exhibition at Wembley in 1924, when it was seen by over one and a half million people. The following year it was lent to the Ideal Home Exhibition at Olympia, where an extra charge of a shilling was made to view it, in aid of the Queen's charitable fund. A portion of each visitor's entrance fee is still donated to charity.

In the adjoining display two remarkable French dolls, France and Marianne, are shown together with part of their extensive wardrobe of clothes and accessories. They were presented to King George VI and Queen Elizabeth for their daughters, the Princesses Elizabeth and Margaret Rose, by the French Government during the 1938 State Visit to France. The dolls' clothes and accessories were designed and made by the leading Parisian fashion houses, including Worth, Lanvin, Cartier, Hermès and Vuitton.

ABOVE: *Queen Mary's Dolls' House: the garden*

RIGHT: *France and Marianne*

Separate publications are available on both Queen Mary's Dolls' House and France and Marianne.

The exceptional collection of drawings housed in the Print Room of the Royal Library has been assembled over the past five hundred years. It includes major works by Holbein, Michelangelo, Raphael, Parmigianino, Guercino, Canaletto and many others. The greatest treasure of the Royal Library is the unparalleled collection of six hundred drawings by Leonardo da Vinci.

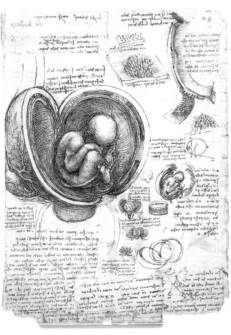

Drawings Gallery

This handsome vaulted undercroft was designed by James Wyatt for George III between 1800 and 1804 to house the new Grand Staircase, an arrangement superseded by Jeffry Wyatville's alterations. The central part of the undercroft, which had formerly housed the stairs, was then vaulted over, and the resulting gothic hall linked the State Entrance to the south and new Grand Staircase to the west. This arrangement ceased in 1867, when Anthony Salvin realigned the Grand Staircase for Queen Victoria. The space is now used as an exhibition gallery for temporary displays from the Royal Collection.

ABOVE RIGHT:
Queen Victoria and Napoleon III in the State Entrance, *1855, watercolour by G. Thomas.*

ABOVE LEFT: *Hans Holbein the Younger,* Sir John Godsalve, c.*1532—4*

LEFT: *Leonardo da Vinci,* A baby in the womb, c.*1511*

NOTE: *To avoid confusion, George IV is referred to in the following pages by his title as King (1820—30). The eldest son of George III and Queen Charlotte, he was created Prince of Wales a week after his birth in 1762, and Prince Regent in 1811.*

China Museum

During the reign of Queen Victoria this room, known as the Museum, was used to display state gifts. The Ionic stone columns date from Hugh May's remodelling in the 1670s. They were reused here during Salvin's work of the 1860s.

Display cabinets

(anticlockwise from right)
Royal Copenhagen dessert service with views of country houses in Denmark, presented to King Edward VII and Queen Alexandra on their marriage in 1863 by the noble ladies of Denmark

Fürstenberg service, *c.*1773. Thought to have been presented to George III by his brother-in-law, the Duke of Brunswick

Etruscan service, Naples, 1785–87. Presented to George III by Ferdinand IV, King of Naples, in 1787

Rockingham service, 1830–37. Commissioned by William IV

Staffordshire (Daniel) service, *c.*1826–30. Made for William IV when Duke of Clarence

Worcester service, 1830. Commissioned by William IV

Worcester Harlequin service, *c.*1807–16. Made for George IV

Coalport service, 1818. Presented to Edward, Duke of Kent, by the City of London, on his marriage

Tournai service, *c.*1787. Made for the Duke of Orléans. Acquired by George IV

Sèvres service, 1764–70. Acquired by George IV

Examples from several Meissen services, *c.*1750

Flora Danica service, Royal Copenhagen. Presented to King Edward VII and Queen Alexandra on their marriage in 1863 by the King and Queen of Denmark

WORCESTER DESSERT SERVICE

This richly gilded service was commissioned by William IV in 1830 and took two years to complete. It is decorated with the royal arms and the insignia of the Orders of the Garter, Thistle, St Patrick, Bath, St Michael, St George and the Guelphic Order. It is used to ornament the table for the annual luncheon of the Knights and Ladies of the Garter.

ROCKINGHAM SERVICE

Probably the most ambitious porcelain service ever made by a British factory, this service was ordered by William IV on his accession in 1830 but not delivered until 1837, the year of his death. It was first used by his young niece Queen Victoria. The proprietors of the Rockingham Works in South Yorkshire were ruined by the expense. The decoration of individual pieces celebrates Britain's maritime achievements and expanding Empire, with scenes of India and the Caribbean, and wonderfully modelled pineapples, sugar cane, exotic fruits, coral and shells. Parts of the service are displayed during state banquets.

ETRUSCAN SERVICE

Presented to George III by Ferdinand IV of Naples in 1787 and made at the royal porcelain factory in Naples, the service was intended to show off the collection of ancient vases in the Neapolitan royal collection. Individual vases were painted on the plates and antique forms were ingeniously adapted for modern uses such as tureens or bottle coolers.

FAR LEFT: *Plate from the Tournai service, c.1787*

The massive statue of George IV dominating the half-landing was completed by Sir Francis Chantrey (1781–1841) in 1832, two years after the King's death, but dated 1830 to ensure that the sculptor was paid. Also displayed on the landing are some Tudor gun-shields and the laid-up colours of disbanded English and Irish regiments.

Grand Staircase

The site of the Grand Staircase was originally an internal courtyard known as Brick Court. Jeffry Wyatville added the glazed gothic lantern roof, which survived the realignment of the staircase in the 1860s. The trophies of arms and armour which line the walls are based on an arrangement made for William IV in the 1830s.

All visitors to the State Apartments, whether members of the public or heads of state, ascend this magnificent staircase to begin their tour. Heads of state and guests of The Queen enter via the State Entrance in the Quadrangle and approach the staircase from its southern side.

The two diminutive suits of armour on either side of the stairs were made for James I's son Henry, Prince of Wales (1594–1612), when he was around 14 years old. Henry, elder brother of Charles I, had a particular love of chivalry. The second suit was a gift from the King of France in 1607.

Grand Vestibule

This space has changed dramatically over the past three centuries. In the late seventeenth century it housed the richly decorated Queen's Great Staircase that led from the ground-floor entrance up to the Queen's apartments. The remarkable plaster fan-vaulted ceiling and lantern are among the few survivors of James Wyatt's work for George III, undertaken between 1800 and 1814 when the Queen's Stair was replaced by a new Great Staircase. The cipher of William IV was added to the ceiling after the stairs were demolished and the Grand Vestibule was created by Wyatt's nephew, Jeffry Wyatville.

The marble statue of Queen Victoria that now dominates the room has been displayed here since its completion in 1872. Its

THE MUSKET BALL THAT KILLED LORD NELSON

Nelson was struck in the left shoulder while on the deck of HMS *Victory* during the Battle of Trafalgar in 1805. The ball was removed by the ship's surgeon shortly after Nelson's death and made into a pendant locket which was later presented to Queen Victoria.

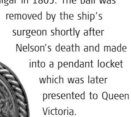

BELOW: *Door lock by William Walls, presented to George III in 1765. The lock incorporates two pistols designed to fire in the event of tampering.*

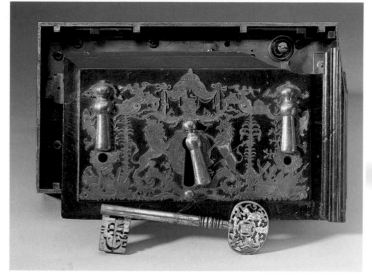

success led to many further royal commissions from the sculptor, Joseph Edgar Boehm. The gothic canopy and showcases were installed in 1888 to display some of the thousands of gifts presented to Queen Victoria on her Golden Jubilee from all corners of the Empire. They now hold an important and disparate group of arms and relics, the majority from the collection of George IV.

TIPU SULTAN

In the central case on the western wall are relics and arms and armour from Tipu, Sultan of Mysore's magnificent palace at Seringapatam in southern India. Known as the Tiger of Mysore, Tipu was a ferocious opponent of the British in India. His defeat and death in 1799 ended years of conflict and prevented an alliance with Napoleon. The life-size tiger's head from Tipu's throne, made of gold with rock crystal teeth, was presented to William IV by the East India Company in 1831.

Pictures

John Vanderbank (1694–1739), *George I on horseback*, 1726

David Morier (1705/6–70), *George II on horseback*, c.1745

Arms, armour and relics (*in display cases, clockwise from left*)
Case 1: Relics of Tipu Sultan, King of Mysore (c.1745–99), taken after the fall of Seringapatam in 1799; gifts of King Mongkut of Siam to Queen Victoria, 1857

Case 2: African, South American and Oriental arms and trophies, including crowns from India, Ethiopia and Ecuador

Cases 3-4: European firearms, including sporting guns, mainly 18th century

Case 5: Trophy of European swords, 17th-18th centuries

Case 6: The musket ball that killed Lord Nelson at the Battle of Trafalgar in 1805, and arms and relics associated with Napoleon, including his scarlet cloak taken after the Battle of Waterloo

Case 7: Three embroidered velvet robes and a surcoat and stole reputedly used by George IV at his coronation in Hanover in 1821, and

a group of sabretaches and pouches from Hussar regiments

Sculpture
Bronze relief, *Rudolph II introducing the Liberal Arts into Bohemia*, by Adriaen de Vries (c.1556–1626), 1609. Purchased by George IV (*see right*)

Marble statue of Queen Victoria with her collie, Sharp, by Sir J.E. Boehm (1834–1890), marble, c.1869–72

Marble busts of Charles I and William III, late 17th century. Acquired by Queen Elizabeth in 1937

Lobby to the Grand Vestibule

Furniture
Two of Queen Charlotte's sedan chairs, leather-covered wood with gilt-metal decoration. The chair on the right was made in 1763 by Samuel Vaughan, with mounts by D.N. Anderson

Display cabinets
Two cases containing equipment of the 10th Light Dragoons, including George IV's jacket and helmet as Colonel of the Regiment (1793–1819)

Waterloo Chamber

This vast room was designed by Jeffry Wyatville for George IV but completed in the reign of his successor William IV. It was built in tribute to the success of the forces of Great Britain, Austria, Prussia and Russia at the Battle of Waterloo in June 1815, when Napoleon Bonaparte was finally defeated. The new room filled in an open court that had survived since the thirteenth century. From the seventeenth century it was known as Horn Court on account of an exceptionally large pair of antlers that were hung there. Hugh May built a staircase, known as the King's Stairs, behind a grandiose façade across the eastern end of the courtyard, as the principal entrance to Charles II's apartments. Visitors crossed the open courtyard at ground-floor level and ascended the stairs to the King's Guard Chamber (now the Grand Reception Room). Open colonnades decorated with baroque wall paintings and gilded statues ran around the sides of the courtyard.

The panelled walls of the Waterloo Chamber are applied with limewood carvings, most of which date from the 1680s, carved by Grinling Gibbons (1648–1721) and his assistants. They were salvaged from the former royal chapel during its demolition in the 1820s. The ingenious roof, decorated by the firm of Crace, has a raking clerestory reminiscent of a ship's timbers. The cut-glass 'gasoliers' by F. & C. Osler were added in 1862, and the 'Elizabethan' fretwork decoration above the panelling in 1881. The Indian carpet was woven for this room by the inmates of Agra prison for Queen Victoria's Golden Jubilee, finally reaching Windsor in 1894. Thought to be the largest seamless carpet in existence, it weighs 2 tonnes; during the 1992 fire it took fifty soldiers to roll it up and move it to safety. The room itself was spared by the thickness of the medieval wall dividing it from St George's Hall.

The Garter Luncheon, given by The Queen for the Knights and Ladies of the Garter, is held here each June. The table is set for fifty to sixty guests with magnificent gilt dining silver from George IV's Grand Service and the Worcester porcelain service normally displayed in the China Museum, and the guests are entertained by a band which plays on the balcony.

Watercolour design by Frederick Crace for the roof of the Waterloo Chamber, 1835

A performance of Les Misérables, *given in the Waterloo Chamber in 2004 for the visit of President Jacques Chirac.*

Pictures

North Wall

Upper level:
Sir Thomas Lawrence (1769–1830), *Louis-Antoine, Duke of Angoulême*, 1825

William Corden (1797–1867), *Frederick William, Duke of Brunswick*, 1848

Sir Thomas Lawrence (1769–1830), *Prince Leopold of Saxe-Coburg, later King of the Belgians*, 1821

Lower level:
Sir Thomas Lawrence (1769–1830), *Adolphus, Duke of Cambridge*, 1818

Sir Thomas Lawrence (1769–1830), *Robert Banks Jenkinson, 2nd Earl of Liverpool*, c.1820

Sir David Wilkie (1785–1841), *William IV*, 1832

Sir Thomas Lawrence (1769–1830), *George III*, c.1820

Studio of Sir Thomas Lawrence, *George IV*, c.1820

Sir Thomas Lawrence (1769–1830), *Robert Stewart, Viscount Castlereagh*, c.1817

Sir Thomas Lawrence (1769–1830), *Frederick, Duke of York*, 1816

East Wall

Upper level:
Robert McInnes (1801–86), *General Sir James Kempt*, 1836

Sir Thomas Lawrence (1769–1830), *Matvei Ivanovitch, Count Platov*, 1814

Sir Thomas Lawrence (1769–1830), *Arthur Wellesley, 1st Duke of Wellington*, 1814–15

Sir Thomas Lawrence (1769–1830), *Field Marshal Gebhardt von Blücher*, 1814

James Lonsdale (1777–1839), *Sir William Congreve*, c.1805–10

Lower level:
Sir Thomas Lawrence (1769–1830), *Charles William, Baron von Humboldt*, 1828

After Sir Thomas Lawrence, *George Canning*, c.1830

Sir Thomas Lawrence (1769–1830), *Henry, 3rd Earl Bathurst*, c.1820

Sir Thomas Lawrence (1769–1830), *Ernest Frederick, Count Münster*, 1820

South Wall

Upper level:
Sir Martin Archer Shee (1769–1850), *Henry Paget, 2nd Earl of Uxbridge and 1st Marquess of Anglesey*, 1836

Sir Thomas Lawrence (1769–1830), *Alexander Ivanovitch, Prince Chernichev*, 1818

Nicaise de Keyser (1813–1887), *William II, King of the Netherlands, when Prince of Orange*, 1846

Lower level:
Sir Thomas Lawrence (1769–1830), *Ercole, Cardinal Consalvi*, 1819

Sir Thomas Lawrence (1769–1830), *Charles Augustus, Prince Hardenberg*, 1818

Sir Thomas Lawrence (1769–1830), *Tsar Alexander I of Russia*, 1814–18

Sir Thomas Lawrence (1769–1830), *The Emperor Francis I of Austria*, 1818–19

Sir Thomas Lawrence (1769–1830), *Frederick William III of Prussia*, 1814–18

Sir Thomas Lawrence (1769–1830), *Charles Robert, Count Nesselrode*, 1818

Sir Thomas Lawrence (1769–1830), *Pope Pius VII*, 1819

West Wall

Upper level:
Henry William Pickersgill (1782–1875), *General Viscount Hill*, c.1830

Sir Thomas Lawrence (1769–1830), *Charles X of France*, 1825

Sir Thomas Lawrence (1769–1830), *Charles Philip, Prince Schwarzenberg*, 1819

Sir Thomas Lawrence (1769–1830), *Charles, Archduke of Austria*, 1819

Sir Martin Archer Shee (1769–1850), *Sir Thomas Picton*, 1836

Lower level:
Sir Thomas Lawrence (1769–1830), *John, Count Capo D'Istria*, 1818–19

Sir Thomas Lawrence (1769–1830), *Clemens Lothar Wenzel, Prince Metternich*, 1819

Sir Thomas Lawrence (1769–1830), *Armand Emmanuel, Duke of Richelieu*, 1818

Sir Thomas Lawrence (1769–1830), *General Theodore Petrovich Uvarov*, 1818

Furniture

Mahogany extending dining table by Thomas Dowbiggin, 1846. Made for Queen Victoria

Giltwood sofas in the gothic style, designed by James Wyatt for the Palace of Westminster and made by John Russell and Charles Elliott, 1807

Indian (Agra) carpet, presented to Queen Victoria in 1894

Set of six French gilt-bronze tripod tazzas, early 19th century

A HALL OF FAME

Sir Thomas Lawrence, Britain's leading portraitist, was chosen by George IV to paint many of the victorious allied monarchs, statesmen and commanders. The eastern wall is dominated by the portrait of the Duke of Wellington (*below*), flanked by the aged Marshal Blücher of Prussia and Count Platov, commander of the Cossack cavalry. The portrait of Pope Pius VII (*bottom*) is considered to be one of Lawrence's greatest works.

The State Apartments

The sequence of rooms built for Charles II and his Queen, Catherine of Braganza, between 1675 and 1678 formed the grandest sequence of baroque state apartments in England, with elaborate painted ceilings and panelled walls ornamented with superb carvings by Grinling Gibbons and his assistants. The rooms have been much altered subsequently: the panelling was replaced by silk hangings in George III's reign (renewed many times since), and all but three of the original painted ceilings by Antonio Verrio were renewed under Wyatville's direction in ornamental plaster by Francis Bernasconi. Many of the original cornices, dados and carvings can still be seen.

Ante-Throne Room

This unassuming ante-room was created by Wyatville from the western end of the much larger King's Audience Chamber (also called the King's Privy Chamber).

King's Drawing Room

This was Charles II's withdrawing-room (see pp. 18–19), where he received important visitors and held court assemblies. His Grooms in Waiting slept here. The room marked the divide between the public ante-rooms to the east and the King's private apartments to the west. Courtiers and other 'people of quality' would gather here each morning to pay their respects. Wyatville added the large bay window and the Siena marble chimneypiece, and the room preserves almost nothing of its seventeenth-century appearance. Only the cornice, carved in Grinling Gibbons' workshop, survives from the seventeenth century.

George IV's body lay in state here in 1830. The room was draped with black velvet and lit by candlelight. His niece, Queen Victoria, regularly held theatrical performances here – on a stage erected at the north (window) end.

Ante-Throne Room

Furniture

Pair of giltwood mirrors (originally picture frames), carved with the ciphers of William III and Mary II

Two giltwood side tables with marble tops, 18th and 19th centuries

Rosewood and brass inlaid centre table, early 19th century

Pair of ebony and Boulle marquetry side cabinets, mid-19th century

Tapestries

Two tapestries from the *History of Meleager* series, woven at the Gobelins factory in Paris 1824–33 following earlier designs by Charles Lebrun. Presented to Queen Victoria by King Louis-Philippe in 1843. The subjects are *The Hunt* and *The Death of Meleager*.

BELOW: *Sir Anthony Van Dyck,* St Martin dividing his cloak, *c.1618*

ABOVE: *The King's Drawing Room*

In Queen Victoria's reign the works of single artists were gathered together in three of the principal State Apartments and the rooms renamed accordingly. Hung entirely with works by (or then thought to be by) the great Flemish baroque painter Peter Paul Rubens (1577–1640), this room became the Rubens Room. It was redecorated in 2005–6.

RIGHT: *Verrio's original ceiling in the King's Drawing Room, with Charles II proceeding in Triumph. Engraving by J. Bowles*

Pictures

Studio of Sir Peter Paul Rubens, *Equestrian portrait of Philip II of Spain, c.1620*

Sir Peter Paul Rubens (1577–1640) and studio, *Equestrian portrait of Don Rodrigo Calderón, c.1612*

Sir Peter Paul Rubens (1577–1640) and studio, *Family of Sir Balthazar Gerbier, c.1629–30*

Sir Peter Paul Rubens (1577–1640), *Landscape with St George and the Dragon, c.1630*

Sir Peter Paul Rubens (1577–1640), *The Holy Family with St Francis of Assisi, 1626–8*

Sir Anthony Van Dyck (1599–1641), *St Martin dividing his cloak, c.1618*

Furniture

Pair of Boulle marquetry and lacquer cabinets, 18th and 19th centuries

Pollard elm and giltwood writing table by Jacob Frères, *c.1805*

French lacquer and gilt-bronze cabinet, late 18th and 19th centuries

Pair of English giltwood torchères, *c.1730*

French lacquer and gilt-bronze cabinet by Joseph Baumhauer, *c.1770*. Acquired by George IV in 1825

Set of four giltwood torchères, *c.1840*

French ebony and Boulle marquetry writing table, *c.1710*

Giltwood seat furniture from two sets made for Windsor by Morel & Seddon, *c.1828*. One set with covers embroidered by Frederica, Duchess of York, purchased by George IV in 1827 at the sale of the Duke of York's possessions

Organ clock by Charles Clay, *c.1730*, incorporating a rock crystal and enamel casket by Melchior Baumgartner, Augsburg, dated 1664. At Queen Victoria's request, the Bible used by General Gordon at Khartoum was placed inside the casket after his death *(see right)*

French ebony and lacquer secretaire, early 19th century

French ebony veneered writing desk, late 18th century

Pair of 18th-century gilt-bronze allegorical groups representing Painting and Sculpture. Purchased by George IV in 1827

Persian carpet, early 20th century. Presented to King Edward VII by the Shah of Persia in 1903

Porcelain

Four Chinese blue and white porcelain jars and covers, 17th century

Four candelabra of Chinese blue porcelain with French gilt-bronze mounts, 18th century

Pair of Chinese celadon porcelain vases, mid-18th century

Sculpture

Bronze equestrian group of Henri IV of France, 18th century

Bronze figure of Hercules after Giambologna, 18th century

King's Bedchamber

Charles II used this room for the formal ceremonies of *levée* and *couchée* when, following Louis XIV's example, the King officially rose and went to bed attended by members of the court; as at Versailles, a low balustrade divided the room – as Celia Fiennes put it, 'to secure the bed from the common'. Although he listened to sermons and occasionally dined here, it is thought that Charles II more routinely slept in the small bedchamber next door.

Access to the King's Bedchamber was limited. Here the King met his ministers and other advisers and transacted secret affairs of state. The present appearance of the room is due partly to George III, who first introduced crimson silk hangings in place of the seventeenth-century panelling, and partly to his son George IV. During Wyatville's restoration in the 1820s, the marble chimneypiece designed by Sir William Chambers was removed from Buckingham House (then being transformed into Buckingham Palace) and installed here.

Pictures

Francis Cotes (1726-70), *Queen Charlotte with Charlotte, Princess Royal*, 1767

Canaletto (1697–1768), *Venice: View towards Murano from the Fondamenta Nuove*, c.1750

Sir William Beechey (1753–1839), *Princess Augusta*, c.1802

Canaletto (1697–1768), *Venice: The Grand Canal towards the Bacino, with S. Maria della Salute*, c.1750

Canaletto (1697–1768), *Rome: View of the Colosseum and the Arch of Constantine*, 1743

Over the doors:
Canaletto (1697–1768), *Venice: Caprice view of the courtyard of the Doge's Palace with the Scala dei Giganti*, 1744

Canaletto (1697–1768), *Venice: Caprice view of the Piazzetta with the Horses of S. Marco*, 1743

Furniture

French giltwood 'polonaise' bed, attributed to Georges Jacob, late 18th century

French chest of drawers and pair of corner cupboards with Japanese lacquer panels and gilt-bronze mounts, by Bernard (II) van Risamburgh, c.1750

English mahogany work table made for Queen Charlotte by William Vile, 1763

French patinated and gilt-bronze 'Rape of Europa' clock; case by R. Osmond with a later movement by B.L. Vulliamy, on a musical-box base, mid-18th century

French oval parquetry table by R. Lacroix, c.1770, inset with a Sèvres porcelain plaque dated 1763

Part of a large set of English carved and gilded gesso side chairs, c.1730 and later

Gilt-bronze and white marble allegorical clock by Vulliamy, 1787, with Derby porcelain figure

Pair of French white marble and gilt-bronze vases, late 18th century

Two Chinese celadon porcelain vases mounted as candelabra by Vulliamy for the Royal Pavilion, Brighton, 1819

English rosewood games table, early 19th century

Oval carved and giltwood pier glass, designed by John Yenn, c.1794–5, and carved by Richard Lawrence

French (Savonnerie) carpet, second half of 18th century

Cut-glass chandelier, early 19th century

King's Dressing Room

This small intimate space was Charles II's Little Bedchamber, where he most probably slept. However, the King was often elsewhere; he installed one of his favourites, Louise de Kéroualle, Duchess of Portsmouth, in a suite immediately below, and another, Nell Gwynn, in a large house to the south of the castle.

By 1696 the room was known as the 'king's customary bedchamber'. In the 1830s Wyatville installed the plaster ceiling with the arms and cipher of William IV, anchors and tridents – motifs that refer to the 'Sailor' King's career in the navy before his accession. The room's current name derives from later use as a visiting king's dressing room.

On display here are some of the most important northern Renaissance paintings in the Royal Collection, chiefly dating from the sixteenth century. Over the fireplace is the Dutch artist Marten van Heemskerck's *The Four Last Things,* dated 1565. The title refers to Death, Judgement, Paradise and Hell. On the wall opposite the windows are two small portraits by Hans Holbein the Younger and three by his German compatriot Lucas Cranach the Elder, the latter acquired by Prince Albert in the mid-nineteenth century. The most famous painting in the room is Pieter Breughel the Elder's *The Massacre of the Innocents* on the right-hand wall. It depicts the story from St Matthew's Gospel in which King Herod decreed that all the newborn children of Bethlehem be slaughtered. In the early seventeenth century before the picture entered the Royal Collection, the infant children were painted over and the subject transformed into the sacking of a village.

ABOVE: *Lucas Cranach the Elder,* Apollo and Diana, *c.1530*

BELOW: *Pieter Breughel the Elder,* The Massacre of the Innocents, *c.1565–7*

Pictures

After Hans Holbein the Younger, *Christina of Denmark, Duchess of Milan, c.1540*

Francois Clouet (*c.1510–72*), *Francis II, King of France, when young, c.1560*

Marten van Heemskerck (d.1574), *The Four Last Things,* 1565

Hans Holbein the Younger (1497/8–1543), *William Reskimer, c.1532–3*

Jean Perréal (*c.1455–1530*), *Louis XII, King of France, c.1490*

Lucas Cranach the Elder (1472–1553), *Apollo and Diana, c.1530*

Jan Breughel the Elder (1568–1625), *Adam and Eve in the Garden of Eden,* 1615

Quinten Metsys (1466–1530), *Desiderius Erasmus,* 1517

Jan Gossaert, called Mabuse (1478–1536), *The children of Christian II of Denmark, c.1526*

Hans Holbein the Younger (1497/8–1543), *Derich Born,* 1533

Hendrick van Steenwyck the Younger (1580–1649), *The Liberation of St Peter,* 1619

Hans Baldung Grien (1484/5–1545), *Portrait of a young man with a rosary,* 1509

Lucas Cranach the Elder (1472–1553), *The Judgement of Paris, c.1538–43*

Lucas Cranach the Elder (1472–1553), *Lucretia,* 1530

Jan Breughel the Elder (1568–1625), *A Flemish fair,* 1600

Pieter Breughel the Elder (1525–69), *The Massacre of the Innocents, c.1565–7*

Furniture

French mahogany trellis-back chairs and settee by Georges Jacob, late 18th century, from a set supplied through Dominique Daguerre to George IV

English gilt-bronze chandelier, early 19th century

LEFT: *Agnolo Bronzino,* Portrait of a lady in green, *c.1530, from the collection of Charles I*

King's Closet

The room was created from two smaller rooms for George III in 1804. This was the site of Charles II's Closet – his most private space to which only the King and his trusted servant William Chiffinch had keys. Here, where the King kept some of his most precious treasures, he could escape from court life.

The plaster ceiling was added for William IV in 1833 and incorporates the arms and cipher of his consort, Adelaide of Saxe-Meiningen. Today it contains some of the finest Italian Renaissance paintings in the Royal Collection.

RIGHT TOP: *Giovanni Bellini,* Portrait of a young man, *c.1507*
RIGHT: *Lorenzo Costa,* Portrait of a lady with a lap-dog, *c.1500*

Pictures

Dosso Dossi (1479–1542), *St William,* c.1524

Agnolo Bronzino (1503–72), *Portrait of a lady in green, c.1530*

Andrea del Sarto (1486–1530), *Virgin and Child,* c.1528–30

Follower of Raphael, *Portrait of a young man, c.1510–15*

Girolamo Savoldo (1480–1548/9), *The Virgin adoring the Child with two donors,* c.1528–30

Workshop of Giovanni Bellini, *The Concert,* c.1500

Lorenzo Costa (c.1459/60–1535), *Portrait of a lady with a lap-dog,* c.1500

Giovanni Bellini (1430–1516), *Portrait of a young man,* c.1507

Lorenzo Lotto (c.1480–1556), *Portrait of a man holding a glove,* c.1520

Correggio (before 1494–1534), *Holy Family with St Jerome,* c.1517

Dosso Dossi (1479–1542), *Holy Family,* c.1528–29

Palma Vecchio (before 1510–1528), *A sibyl,* c.1520

Jacopo Bassano (?1510–92), *Journey of Jacob,* c.1560

Francesco Salviati (1510–63), *Virgin and Child with an angel,* c.1555

Parmigianino (1503–40), *Pallas Athena,* c.1531–5

Benozzo Gozzoli (1420–97), *Fall of Simon Magus,* 1461

Giovanni Cariani (1487–1547), *The lovers,* c.1517

Furniture
French lacquer cabinet by Charles Saunier, c.1775

French lacquer cabinet with gilt-bronze mounts, c.1775 and later

Pair of French patinated and gilt-bronze candelabra by F. Rémond, c.1783. Acquired by George IV

Mantel clock by Benjamin Vulliamy, 1789–90, with a Derby biscuit porcelain figure of Euterpe, muse of Music

French chinoiserie mantel clock, c.1745, with later movement by Benjamin Vulliamy

French mahogany trellis-back chairs by Georges Jacob, late 18th century

Sculpture
Bronze equestrian group of Marcus Aurelius after the Antique, 18th century

Porcelain
Pair of Chinese celadon vases with French mounts, c.1750

Queen's Drawing Room

This room was designed by Hugh May as Catherine of Braganza's Withdrawing Room. According to the conventions of the time, it was towards the end of a sequence of apartments designated for her use. Queen Catherine's bedchamber and private apartments originally continued to the west but were incorporated into the Royal Library in the 1830s.

Like the King's apartments, the Queen's Drawing Room was originally hung with tapestry and had a ceiling painted with an assembly of the gods. This was replaced in 1834 with a plaster ceiling loosely based on seventeenth-century designs, incorporating the arms of William IV and Queen Adelaide. During the nineteenth century this room, then called the Picture Gallery, was densely hung with Old Masters. Today some of the finest Tudor and Stuart royal portraits in the Royal Collection are hung here.

LEFT: *Chinese porcelain cistern with French mounts, formerly belonging to Madame de Pompadour*

CHARLES I IN THREE POSITIONS

Queen Henrietta Maria obtained the permission of the Pope for his sculptor Gianlorenzo Bernini to make a portrait of Charles I, but he was not permitted to travel to the English court. Instead, the King sat to Van Dyck for a portrait (*below*) to act as a model for the sculptor in Rome. The marble bust duly arrived in London in 1637 to universal praise. It was sold under Cromwell's regime, returned after the Restoration, but was destroyed in the Whitehall Palace fire in 1698.

Pictures

Marcus Gheeraerts the Younger (1561–1635), *Queen Anne, Consort of James I*, 1614

Hans Holbein the Younger (1497/8–1543), *Sir Henry Guildford*, 1527

Joos van Cleve (1485–1540/1), *Henry VIII*, c.1535

Girolamo da Treviso (*fl.* 1524–44), *A Protestant allegory*, c.1536

Attributed to Guillim Scrots, *Edward VI*, c.1546

Robert Peake (d.1626), *Henry, Prince of Wales, in the hunting field*, c.1606–7

Anthonis Mor (1517–75), *Mary I*, c.1570

Hans Eworth (before 1540–1573), *Henry Stewart, Lord Darnley, and his brother Charles Stewart, Earl of Lennox*, c.1562

Attributed to Hans Eworth, *Elizabeth I and the Three Goddesses*, 1569

Hans Holbein the Younger (1497/8–1543), *Thomas Howard, 3rd Duke of Norfolk*, 1538–9

William Wissing (1653–87), *William III when Prince of Orange*, c.1685

Paul van Somer (1576–1621), *James I*, c.1620

John Riley (1646–92), *Prince George of Denmark, husband of Queen Anne*, c.1687

Paul van Somer (1576–1621), *Queen Anne, consort of James I*, 1617

William Wissing (1653–87), *Mary II when Princess of Orange*, 1685

Sir Peter Paul Rubens (1577–1640), *Self-portrait*, 1622

Sir Peter Lely (1608–88), *Princess Mary, later Mary II*, c.1672

Sir Anthony Van Dyck (1599–1641), *Charles I in three positions*, c.1635–6

Sir Peter Paul Rubens (1577–1640), *Portrait of a woman*, c.1628–30

Leonard Knyff (1650–1722), *A view of Windsor Castle from the north*, c.1705

William Dobson (1611–46), *Charles II when Prince of Wales*, 1644

Adriaen Hanneman (1601–71), *William III when Prince of Orange*, 1664

Sir Anthony Van Dyck (1599–1641), *Queen Henrietta Maria*, c.1632

Simon Verelst (1618–88), *Mary of Modena, Duchess of York*, c.1635. The Duchess is wearing an expensively embroidered male costume

Furniture

English walnut and rosewood 'seaweed' marquetry bureau inlaid with the cipher of William III, by Gerrit Jensen, late 17th century

English marquetry cabinet veneered with brass, pewter, ebony and other woods, with the cipher of William III, by Gerrit Jensen, c.1695

Pair of English giltwood candle stands, c.1740. Purchased by Queen Elizabeth in 1947. Formerly at Ditchley Park, Oxfordshire

Astronomical clock by Jakob Mayr, Augsburg, c.1700

Part of a large set of English carved and gilded gesso side chairs, c.1730 and later

French ebony cabinet-on-stand, carved with representations of the young Louis XIV and scenes from contemporary literature, c.1650

Ebony and giltwood centre table by Morel & Seddon, c.1828

Giltwood pier table with *scagliola* (imitation marble) top, by Marsh & Tatham, 1814. Made for George IV

English giltwood pier glass, early 19th century

Pair of French marble and gilt-bronze candelabra, late 18th century

French gilt-bronze mantel clock, case by R. Osmond, movement by J. Lepaute, c.1780

Pair of rouge marble and gilt-bronze candelabra, late 18th century

English gilt-bronze chandelier by Hancock & Rixon, 1828

Porcelain

Chinese blue porcelain cistern with French gilt-bronze mounts, mid-18th century. Belonged to Mme de Pompadour

Pair of Chinese blue and gold porcelain vases and covers with French gilt-bronze mounts, early 18th century

Chinese *famille rose* punch bowl, mid-18th century

Pair of Chinese white porcelain vases, presented to Queen Victoria on her Diamond Jubilee (1897) by the Emperor of China

Robert Peake, Henry, Prince of Wales, in the hunting field, *c.1606–7*

Hans Holbein the Younger, Sir Henry Guildford, *1527*

King's Dining Room

This was Charles II's dining room, and the ceiling – one of
three by Antonio Verrio that remain from the 1680s – is
painted with a banquet of the gods. The room originally
overlooked Brick Court, which was open to the sky until the
1820s. The present fenestration dates from Salvin's
reconstruction of the Grand Staircase in the 1860s. The
remarkable limewood carvings are by Grinling Gibbons and his
assistant Henry Phillips. The garlands of fruit, flowers and game
echo the painted decoration; the palm fronds over the alcoves
are further salvage from May's chapel, destroyed in the 1820s.

The King's Dining Room lies between the King's and Queen's
apartments so that both the King and Queen could eat here.
The alcoves were intended for the use of servants and
musicians; the skylights were added in the 1860s.

ABOVE: *Turkey painted
by Antonio Verrio in the
cove of the ceiling.*

RIGHT: *Limewood
carving by Grinling
Gibbons, 1680.*

Pictures

John Riley (1646–92), *Bridget Holmes*, 1686

(over the fireplace) Jacob Huysmans (1633–80), *Catherine of Braganza*, 1664

Sir Godfrey Kneller (1646–1723), *Michael Alphonsus Shen Fu-Tsung, 'The Chinese Convert'*, 1687

John Michael Wright (1623–1700), *John Lacy*, c.1668–70. An actor, Lacy is shown in three different roles

Furniture

French ebony and Boulle marquetry secretaire, the base c.1710, the upper part c.1770, by E. Levasseur. Bought by George IV, 1812

Pair of English giltwood torchères, c.1730

English ebony and Boulle marquetry breakfront cabinet, early 19th century

Collection of Chinese jade carvings, 18th-19th centuries

Pair of English giltwood pier tables with marble tops, attributed to Jean Pelletier, c.1699

Pair of English giltwood pier glasses, c.1740, with the added cipher of Queen Anne

Pair of English giltwood pier glasses, c.1740

French ebony and Boulle marquetry drop-front secretaire, late 18th century

French Boulle marquetry pedestal clock, late 17th century, with 19th-century movement by B.L. Vulliamy. Purchased by George IV, 1820

Two English walnut and floral marquetry side tables, late 17th century

Six gilt-metal wall sconces with cipher of Charles II, 19th century

Ebony medicine cabinet with silver-gilt mounts, Augsburg, early 17th century, on a later stand

Boulle marquetry mantel clock, late 17th century, with 19th-century movement by B.L. Vulliamy

Ebony bracket clock by Thomas Tompion, late 17th century

English needlework casket, c.1680

English silver-mounted marquetry bellows, late 17th century. Traditionally said to have belonged to Nell Gwynn

Tapestries

Two Brussels panels with the arms of William III and Mary II, designed by Daniel Marot, c.1690. Purchased by Queen Mary, 1914

Porcelain

Two pairs of Chinese porcelain *famille verte* baluster vases, 17th century

Group of Japanese *kakiemon* porcelain vases and square bottles, c.1700, some with 18th-century French gilt-bronze mounts

Japanese Imari porcelain baluster vase, c.1700, with later French gilt-bronze mounts

Four Chinese porcelain long-necked bottles, c.1700

Pair of Japanese porcelain candlesticks, late 17th century, mounted with French gilt-bronze candelabra, late 18th century

Sculpture

Terracotta bust of Charles II, ?late 17th century

French bronze equestrian group of Henri IV, early 19th century

Italian bronze statuette of a faun, 16th century

Bronze group of a faun and sleeping nymph after Giambologna, 18th century

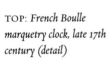

TOP: *French Boulle marquetry clock, late 17th century (detail)*

ABOVE: *Japanese porcelain vase, c.1700*

BRIDGET HOLMES

Bridget Holmes was a 'necessary woman', whose responsibilities included the disposal of the contents of chamber pots. She is depicted at the age of 96. She died in her centenary year, having served in four reigns. The painting was probably commissioned by James II and is without parallel in its grandeur as a portrait of a servant.

'THE CHINESE CONVERT'

Shen Fu-Tsung was one of a party of Chinese who left Macao in 1681 to travel to Europe at the invitation of the Procurator of the Jesuit Order in Rome. In 1687–8 he helped to catalogue Chinese texts in the Bodleian Library at Oxford.

Queen's Ballroom

Built as a dancing chamber for Catherine of Braganza, this remained the principal ballroom in the castle until the completion of the Grand Reception Room and Waterloo Chamber in the 1830s. The room was remodelled by Wyatville, who replaced Verrio's ceiling painting, *Charles II giving freedom to Europe*, and removed the oak panelling. The chimneypiece was moved here from the former Queen's Bedchamber following the incorporation of that room into the Royal Library under William IV. The magnificent glass chandeliers were hung during the reign of Queen Victoria. Also at this time the room was first hung exclusively with portraits by Anthony Van Dyck, an arrangement that continues.

'HUNTING NEGRESS' CLOCK

This clock was purchased from its maker J.-A. Lépine by George IV in 1790. On pulling the right earring the time is indicated in the eye sockets – hours in the left, minutes in the right. A small clockwork organ in the base is activated by pulling the left earring. The organ plays a number of tunes popular in 18th-century France, including operatic airs by Gluck.

Pictures

Sir Anthony Van Dyck (1599–1641), *Charles I in robes of state*, 1636

Sir Anthony Van Dyck (1599–1641), *Portrait of a woman*, c.1634–5

Sir Anthony Van Dyck (1599–1641), *Thomas Killigrew and ?William, Lord Crofts*, 1638

Sir Anthony Van Dyck (1599–1641), *George, 2nd Duke of Buckingham, and his brother Lord Francis Villiers*, 1635

Sir Anthony Van Dyck (1599–1641), *Lady Mary Villiers, Duchess of Richmond, as St Agnes*, c.1637

Sir Anthony Van Dyck (1599–1641), *The three eldest children of Charles I*, 1635

Sir Anthony Van Dyck (1599–1641), *Beatrice of Cusance, Princess of Cantecroix and Duchess of Lorraine*, c.1635

Sir Anthony Van Dyck (1599–1641), *The five eldest children of Charles I*, 1637

Furniture

Pair of English Boulle marquetry writing tables by Louis Le Gaigneur. Purchased by George IV, 1815

Pair of French corner cupboards with Japanese lacquer panels and gilt-bronze mounts, mid-18th century. Purchased by George IV, 1829

French giltwood seat furniture by Georges Jacob, c.1785. Supplied by Dominique Daguerre to George IV for Carlton House

---

LEFT: *Sir Anthony Van Dyck,* Thomas Killigrew and ?William, Lord Crofts, *1638*

BELOW: *Sir Anthony Van Dyck,* The five eldest children of Charles I, *1637*

Two ebony cabinets with Japanese lacquer panels, one French, c.1770, the other made to match by Morel & Hughes, 1812

English silver mirror, c.1670

French gilt-bronze mantel clock by J.-A. Lépine, 1790

English silver table and mirror by Andrew Moore, 1699. Made for William III at Kensington Palace

Pair of silver-mounted cabinets veneered with cocus wood, c.1665. Probably made for Queen Henrietta Maria. Presented to King George V by Lord Rothschild, 1910

English silver pier glass, c.1670. Made for Charles II

Set of three English cut-glass chandeliers, c.1800

Seven silver sconces embossed with Garter badges, c.1680

Three porphyry vases with French gilt-bronze mounts, c.1780

Pair of French gilt-bronze perfume burners with rouge marble bases, early 19th century

Two green marble vases with French gilt-bronze mounts, c.1780

Pair of French Boulle marquetry torchères with gilt-bronze mounts, c.1700. Purchased by George IV

Pair of Boulle marquetry octagonal tables by Thomas Parker, early 19th century

Porcelain

Pair of porcelain tureens and covers with gilt-bronze mounts, 19th century

SILVER FURNITURE

The late seventeenth-century silver furniture is an exceptionally rare survival of a fashion started by Louis XIV at Versailles. The Royal Collection originally had six sets of silver mirrors and tables, together with many wall sconces, chandeliers and sets of fireplace furniture. Such extremely expensive pieces were among the ultimate symbols of prestige and power. Many sets were later melted for the value of their silver.

Queen's Audience Chamber

This room and the adjoining Queen's Presence Chamber retain their painted ceilings, panelling, and carvings by Grinling Gibbons and his assistants, and evoke the original appearance of the King's and Queen's apartments. Antonio Verrio's ceiling depicts Catherine of Braganza in a chariot being drawn by swans towards a temple of virtue.

The white marble chimneypiece dates from the 1730s.

Pictures

Gerrit van Honthorst (1590–1656), *William II, Prince of Orange,* c.1640

Gerrit van Honthorst (1590–1656), *Frederick Henry, Prince of Orange,* 1631

British School, *Mary, Queen of Scots,* c.1620

Furniture

Two Chinese lacquer cabinets, late 17th century, on English giltwood tables, c.1730

Giltwood firescreen with Beauvais tapestry panel by Michel Vellaud, 1815

Flemish ebony cabinet-on-stand with gilt-bronze mounts, late 17th century and later

Pair of English giltwood pier tables, c.1760. Purchased by Queen Mary, 1932. Formerly at Chesterfield House, London

Pair of English giltwood pier glasses, early 19th century

Ebony cabinet by A.-L. Bellangé, c.1820, incorporating 17th-century Florentine *pietra dura* (hardstone) panels of flowers and dwarfs. Purchased by George IV, 1825

Part of a set of English carved and gilded gesso side chairs, c.1730 and later

Patinated and gilt-bronze mantel clock with palm tree and figures, by Justin Vulliamy, late 18th century

Pair of bronze lamps by Justin Vulliamy, 1811. Purchased by George IV for Carlton House

Pair of English giltwood x-frame armchairs, attributed to Henry Williams, 1737

Tapestries

Three Gobelins panels from the *History of Esther* series after J.F. de Troy, 1779–87:
*Coronation of Esther
Triumph of Mordecai
Toilet of Esther*
Purchased by George IV, 1825

Porcelain

Two pairs of Japanese Imari porcelain vases and covers, late 17th century

Two pairs of large Chinese blue and white porcelain vases and covers, c.1700

Pair of French white porcelain and gilt-bronze candelabra, late 18th century

Garniture of three Delft blue and white pottery vases and covers, c.1700

Pair of Chinese blue porcelain vases and covers with gilt decoration, mid-18th century

Tapestries would have been hung in all of the King's and Queen's apartments in Charles II's time. Because they were enormously costly, they would only be exposed to light when the King and Queen were in residence. The tapestries here and in the Queen's Presence Chamber were acquired by George IV in the 1820s.

RIGHT: *Detail of the chimneypiece*

Queen's Presence Chamber

The Presence Chamber was the most accessible and therefore most public of the Queen's apartments. It was also used as a waiting room for visitors. The painted ceiling depicts Catherine of Braganza seated under a canopy held by zephyrs, while figures of Envy and Sedition retreat before the outstretched Sword of Justice.

The marble chimneypiece was designed by Robert Adam for Queen Charlotte's Saloon at Buckingham House. In 1789 the clock was added, with a movement by B.L. Vulliamy and marble figures by John Bacon.

Pictures
After Pierre Mignard, *Elizabeth Charlotte, Princess Palatine, Duchess of Orléans, with her son Philip, and her daughter, Elizabeth,* c.1660

Over the doors:
After Sir Peter Lely, *Frances Stuart, Duchess of Richmond and Lennox,* c.1678–80

Edmund Lily (d.1716), *William Henry, Duke of Gloucester,* 1698. The only one of Queen Anne's fourteen children to survive early infancy, he died at Windsor shortly after his eleventh birthday in 1700

Furniture
Eight Roman giltwood armchairs with embroidered velvet covers, early 18th century. Purchased by George IV, 1827

Pair of Boulle and lacquer cabinets, 18th and 19th centuries

Pair of English giltwood pier tables, c.1760. Purchased by Queen Mary from Chesterfield House in 1932. Probably originally from Stowe, Buckinghamshire

Two English carved and gilded gesso torchères, early 18th century

Giltwood firescreen with Beauvais tapestry panel, late 18th century

Pair of English giltwood pier glasses, early 19th century

Two Chinese celadon porcelain vases mounted as candelabra by Vulliamy for the Royal Pavilion, Brighton, 1819

English rosewood and brass inlaid library table, c.1820

Persian wool carpet, late 19th century

Four French Boulle marquetry pedestals, c.1770

Porcelain
Chinese celadon porcelain dish, 14th century, with French gilt-bronze mounts, c.1730

Chinese celadon vases with French gilt-bronze mounts, 18th-19th centuries

Sculpture
White marble bust of George Frederick Handel, by Louis-François Roubiliac, 1739

White marble bust of the Duke of Villars, by A. Coysevox (1640–1720), 1718

Two French bronze groups of the Rape of the Sabines, after Giambologna, 18th century

White marble bust of Marshal Vauban, by A. Coysevox (1640–1720), 1706

White marble bust of Field Marshal Lord Ligonier by Louis-François Roubiliac (?1705–62), mid-18th century

Tapestries
Four Gobelins panels from the *History of Esther* series after de Troy, 1779–87: *Banquet of Esther Disdain of Mordecai Esther supplicates for the lives of her people Judgement of Haman*

LEFT: *The Queen's Guard Chamber, lithograph by Joseph Nash, 1848.*

Queen's Guard Chamber

From the late seventeenth century the Queen's Guard Chamber marked the entrance to the Queen's apartments. Visitors ascended the Queen's Stair on the site of the adjoining Grand Vestibule. Here the Yeomen of the Guard stopped unauthorised people from progressing further. Charles II specified that 'all persons or gentlemen of quality and good fortune' and 'all wives and daughters of the nobility' should be allowed to pass into the Presence Chamber.

As it now appears, the Guard Chamber is the work of Wyatville, who enlarged the room by adding the bay to the south over the State Entrance portico. This provides views across the Quadrangle to the George IV Gateway, beyond which the Long Walk stretches south. The decorative displays of arms on the walls are simplified versions of seventeenth-century arrangements of standard-issue weaponry. In the display cases are examples of more ornate arms and armour, many of which came from George IV's collection at Carlton House.

HORATIO NELSON

The Guard Chamber is dominated by Sir Francis Chantrey's colossal marble bust of Admiral Lord Nelson, commissioned for this room by William IV and completed in 1835. The King had served with Nelson in the Royal Navy. The bust was originally displayed on a pedestal made from a section of HMS *Victory's* battle-scarred foremast.

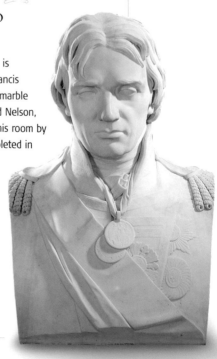

ABOVE: *Bronze bust of Philip II, by Leone Leoni, c.1555.*

RENT BANNERS

The replica French flags over the busts of the 1st Dukes of Marlborough and Wellington are offered each year by their descendants as quit-rents for their estates at Blenheim and Stratfield Saye, which were presented by the grateful nation following their victories over the French. The Duke of Marlborough presents the Bourbon fleur-de-lis flag on the anniversary of the 1st Duke's victory at the Battle of Blenheim in 1704, and the Duke of Wellington presents the Republican tricolour on the anniversary of Waterloo in 1815.

Pictures

Over the fireplace: Joachim Kayser and Johannes Anton von Klyher, *Frederick, Prince of Wales, on horseback,* 1727

Spanish School, *Portrait of a Spanish nobleman,* 16th century

Furniture

Coronation thrones of Jacobean design made by Morris & Co. for King George V and Queen Mary, and copied from a chair at Knole in Kent. Used in the second part of the coronation, 22 June 1911

Throne with the arms of HRH The Duke of Edinburgh, by Beresford & Hicks

Oak thrones of King George V, Queen Mary and Edward, Prince of Wales. Made by Morris & Co. for the investiture of the Prince of Wales in 1911

Coronation thrones made by Howard & Sons for King George V and Queen Mary and copied from a late 17th-century chair at Knole. Used in the first part of the coronation in 1911

The Waterloo Elm armchair, made by Thomas Chippendale the Younger from an elm growing on the field of Waterloo. Presented to George IV in 1821

Gilt-bronze chandelier by W. & G. Perry, 1828

Arms and armour

Trophies of firearms, armour and edged weapons, English, 18th-19th centuries

Guidon of The Queen's Royal Irish Hussars (a guidon is the name given to the flag of a light cavalry regiment)

Colour of the Sovereign's Company of the Grenadier Guards

Japanese Samurai short sword, c.1420

Surrendered by Field Marshal Count Terauchi to the Supreme Allied Commander, South-East Asia (Lord Louis Mountbatten) to mark the end of the war in the Far East, 1945

Display cabinets containing European arms and armour, mainly from the collection of George IV at Carlton House
(clockwise from left):

Case 1: A 17th-century Italian child's half-armour and a display of 18th- and 19th-century small swords

Case 2: Swords and daggers, including a dress sword with a mid-17th-century Dutch carved ivory hilt

Case 3: Firearms, including several Scottish Highland pistols (known as tacks), 1780–1800; and a pair of flintlock pistols by Diemar, c.1780, with inlaid relief decoration to the stocks

Case 4: Includes a half-armour presented to Charles I when Prince of Wales, by Charles Emanuel of Savoy

Sculpture

White marble bust of Admiral Lord Nelson by Sir Francis Chantrey (1781–1841), 1835

Bronze bust of Admiral Lord Nelson by Anne Seymour Damer (1749–1828), 1828

Bronze bust of Philip II, King of Spain, by Leone Leoni (1509–90), c.1555. Purchased by George IV, 1825

Patinated lead equestrian group of William Augustus, Duke of Cumberland, attributed to Henry Cheere, mid-18th century

Bronze bust of Emperor Charles V by Leone Leoni (1509–90), mid-16th century. Purchased by George IV in 1825

Bronze bust of Ferdinand, Duke of Alba, by Leone Leoni (1509–90), mid-16th century. Purchased by George IV in 1825

Bronze bust of Enea Caprara by Massimiliano Soldani-Benzi (1656–1753), c.1695

White marble bust of Sir Winston Churchill by Oscar Nemon (1906–85), 1956. Commissioned by HM The Queen

White marble bust of John Churchill, 1st Duke of Marlborough, by John Henning (1801–57), early 19th century

White marble bust of Arthur, 1st Duke of Wellington, by Sir Francis Chantrey (1781–1841), 1835

Metalwork

Silver-plated replica of the silver-gilt 'Shield of Achilles' designed by John Flaxman, 1820s

Silver, gold and enamel shield, designed by P. von Cornelius, 1842–7. A christening present to the future King Edward VII from his godfather, King Frederick William IV of Prussia

St George's Hall

This magnificent space, measuring 56 by 9 metres (185 by 30 feet) was created for George IV by Wyatville, who combined two adjacent spaces, St George's Hall and the Royal Chapel, to form one long apartment. Both rooms had magnificent baroque murals and ceilings by Verrio and carvings by Grinling Gibbons, all of which was dismantled by Wyatville. The painted ceiling was replaced with plain plasterwork studded with the coats of arms of all the Knights of the Garter since the foundation of the Order in 1348, with grained plaster ribs at intervals.

During the fire of 20 November 1992, the ceiling, roof and east end wall were entirely destroyed and the remainder of the Hall was seriously damaged. When it came to be restored the decision was taken to replace Wyatville's ceiling with a new hammerbeam roof, designed by Giles Downes of the Sidell Gibson Partnership. Constructed entirely of green oak using medieval carpentry techniques, it is the largest timber roof constructed in the twentieth century. The blank shields on the ceiling are the erased arms of those 'degraded' Knights expelled from the Order at different times. The names of all Knights past and present are inscribed on the panels around the Hall, together with the date of their installation and the corresponding number of their coat of arms.

The screen at the east end, also a new addition, supports carvings of the Queen's Beasts given by the Corporation of London in support of the fire restoration and to mark the Golden Wedding Anniversary of The Queen and The Duke of Edinburgh. The silvered and painted plaster Garter and rose on the gable above was presented by the nations of the Commonwealth. The fifty-three petals represent the member countries. The design was taken from a fifteenth-century lockplate in St George's Chapel.

St George's Hall has had a continuous association with the Order of the Garter for six hundred years. In June each year The Queen, The Duke of Edinburgh and the other twenty-four Knights assemble here before processing to St George's Chapel for their annual service.

The Hall is also used for state banquets, held at the beginning of a State Visit. The dining table, normally kept in the Waterloo Chamber, is extended to its full length of 53 metres (175 feet) and seats 162 people.

Pictures

Sir Anthony Van Dyck (1599–1641), *James I*, c.1635–6

Daniel Mytens (1590–1648), *Charles I*, 1631

Sir Peter Lely (1608–88) and a later hand, *Charles II*, c.1672

Sir Peter Lely (1608–88) and studio, *James II*, c.1665–70

Sir Godfrey Kneller (1646–1723), *Mary II*, 1690

Sir Godfrey Kneller (1646–1723), *William III*, c.1690

Studio of Sir Godfrey Kneller, *Queen Anne*, c.1705

Studio of Sir Godfrey Kneller, *George I*, c.1715

Enoch Seeman (b.1661), *George II*, c.1730

Gainsborough Dupont (1754–97), *George III*, c.1794

Sir Thomas Lawrence (1769–1830), *George IV*, c.1825

Sculpture

Twenty-one marble busts of sovereigns and other royal members of the Order of the Garter:

North Wall
J. M. Rysbrack (1693–1770), *Queen Anne*, c.1710

Louis-François Roubiliac (?1705–62), *George II*, c.1760

John Bacon (1740–99), *George III*, 1775

Sir Francis Chantrey (1781–1841), *George IV*, 1826

Sir Frances Chantrey (1781–1841), *William IV*, 1837

Edward Onslow Ford (1852–1917), *Queen Victoria*, 1898

R.W. Sievier (1794–1865), *Albert, Prince Consort*, 1842

Sidney March (1876–1968), *King Edward VII*, 1902

J.E. Boehm (1834–90), *Alfred, Duke of Edinburgh*, 1879

F.J. Williamson (1833–1920), *Leopold, Duke of Albany*, 1883

F.J. Williamson (1833–1920), *Arthur, Duke of Connaught*, 1885

South Wall
Peter Scheemakers (1691–1781), *Frederick, Prince of Wales*, c.1733

Joseph Nollekens (1737–1823), *William, Duke of Cumberland*, 1814 (copy of a bust by Rysbrack of 1754)

Joseph Nollekens (1737–1823), *Edward, Duke of York*, c.1766

J.C. Lochee (b.1751), *Frederick, Duke of York*, c.1787

William Behnes (1795–1864), *Ernest, Duke of Cumberland*, 1826

William Behnes (1795–1864), *Edward, Duke of Kent*, 1828

Lawrence Macdonald (1799–1878), *Adolphus, Duke of Cambridge*, 1848

William Theed (1804–91), *Augustus Frederick, Duke of Sussex* (posthumous bust), 1881

G. G. Adams (1821–98), *George, Duke of Cambridge*, 1888

W. White (fl.1863–1900) after R. Begas, *Frederick III, King of Prussia*, 1897

Furniture

Massive carved oak chair of state known as Edward III's throne, c.1835

ABOVE: Queen Victoria and Louis-Philippe of France entering St George's Hall for the State banquet, 11 October 1844, *watercolour by Joseph Nash.*

BELOW: *Every year a Christmas tree is set up in St George's Hall.*

Lantern Lobby

This room was created after the 1992 fire on the site of the former private chapel, where the fire broke out. The chapel had been created for Queen Victoria from George IV's Band Room to a somewhat unsatisfactory design by Edward Blore. During the restoration it was decided to relocate the chapel and to allow a processional route between the State and Semi-State Apartments that continue at a right angle to the south. The octagonal Lantern Lobby conveniently turns the axis between the two. It was designed by Giles Downes in a modern gothic style partly inspired by Ely Cathedral and the Abbey of Batalha in Portugal. The columns, vaults and balustrade are constructed from laminated oak, a modern technique which contrasts with that used for the roof of St George's Hall. On the floor, the badge and motto of the Garter are inlaid in British marbles. The deep-red stone that forms the cross in the centre is from Derbyshire. It exists in a very small deposit on the estate of the Duke of Devonshire and is known as 'The Duke's Red'. The altar reredos, damaged in the fire, has been preserved and incorporates an inscribed tablet commemorating the restoration.

SILVER-GILT

The Lantern Lobby was partly conceived as a treasury. In the wall cases are displayed some of the finest examples of gilded silver in the Royal Collection, many of them acquired by George IV. Among the most flamboyant pieces displayed here are the National Cup and the Coronation Cup, both made by the Royal Goldsmiths, Rundell, Bridge & Rundell in the late 1820s. Virtually all the pieces on display are made of silver, covered with a very thin layer of gold.

ABOVE: *Centrepiece by George Wickes, 1745*
LEFT: *Sconce by Robert Smythier, 1686*

Display cases
Large case with mainly English silver gilt-vessels and dishes, 17th-19th centuries, including a centrepiece designed by William Kent and made for Frederick, Prince of Wales, 1745; and a pair of Charles II firedogs adapted for George IV and engraved with his arms

Two cases with a selection of standing cups, English and Continental, 16th-19th centuries

Case with a selection of altar plate from the private chapels of Windsor Castle, Buckingham Palace and the Royal Pavilion, Brighton, English, 17th-19th centuries

Picture
George Weymouth (b.1936), *HRH Prince Philip, Duke of Edinburgh*, 1995

Sculpture
Bronze bust of HM The Queen by the Australian sculptor John Dowie, 1997

Pictures in the corridor
Sir Joshua Reynolds (1723–92), *George III when Prince of Wales* 1759

Allan Ramsay (1713–84), *Elizabeth Albertina, Princess of Mecklenburg* 1769

RIGHT: *The Lantern Lobby*

HENRY VIII'S ARMOUR

This magnificent suit of armour was made at Greenwich around 1540. Several 'exchange' pieces to adapt the armour for the different exercises of the tournament are shown in the Queen's Guard Chamber. The armour records the King's impressive proportions, which were quite exceptional in the sixteenth century.

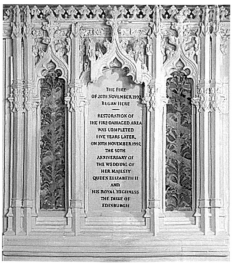

ABOVE: *The reredos of the former private chapel with the inscription commemorating the fire and restoration.*

65

The Semi-State Apartments

This glittering sequence of rooms was created for George IV in the 1820s. Originally built as the King's private apartments, they are now used by The Queen for entertaining and are open to the public only during the winter months.

RIGHT: *The Green Drawing Room*

Following his accession in 1820, George IV decided not to live in the north range, the site of the King's apartments since the twelfth century, preferring the southern and eastern ranges where his mother and sisters had lived. This group of apartments was designed by Wyatville as a sequence of Drawing Rooms, Dining Rooms and Library for the King's private use, and they reflect perfectly George IV's lavish taste. The interiors were furnished and decorated by Morel & Seddon. Some of the fittings and furnishings came from Carlton House, George IV's London home as Prince of Wales and Prince Regent, which was demolished in 1827. The rooms form a superb and unrivalled sequence, widely regarded as the finest and most complete expression of later Georgian taste in Britain.

The Semi-State Apartments were severely damaged by the 1992 fire. They had previously been cleared of most of their contents as part of a long-term rewiring project, an important factor in the decision to restore the rooms to their original condition. The original finishes had become subdued over the intervening 170 years and the restoration project enabled a return to their intended sparkling magnificence.

Green Drawing Room

This was originally planned as a library, flanked by the White Drawing Room to the south (not open to the public) and the Crimson Drawing Room to the north. All three rooms conform to George IV's favourite plan of a long room with a large window bay in the centre at one side. The ceiling here is perhaps Wyatville's most accomplished at Windsor. Although the 1992 fire only damaged the eastern end of the room, the rest was soaked with water. The magnificent carpet, which survived the fire, is now considered too delicate to allow visitors to walk on it. It was specifically designed for this room by Ludwig Grüner for Queen Victoria and Prince Albert and was shown at the Great Exhibition of 1851.

THE LOUIS XVI SERVICE

The display cases contain perhaps the finest Sèvres porcelain dining service ever made, ordered by Louis XVI for his own use at Versailles. Production started in 1783 and a twenty-year production schedule was drawn up by the King himself. It was the most expensive service produced by the Sèvres factory during the eighteenth century. Production ceased abruptly with the King's execution in 1793. The service was auctioned by the Revolutionary Government in 1794 and acquired by George IV in 1810–11.

PASSEMENTERIE

The magnificent curtains with their complex fringing and tassels (*passementerie*) in this and the adjoining rooms are closely based on Morel & Seddon's designs. Each tassel, of silk thread around a carved boxwood core, was made by hand.

Crimson Drawing Room

This, the principal room in the Semi-State Apartments, was severely damaged in the 1992 fire, when the ceiling collapsed and the walls were badly burnt. The steel roof structure expanded in the intense heat and pushed out the eastern wall overlooking the garden, threatening the entire façade with collapse. The restored ceiling incorporates many salvaged fragments of the original. George IV's decorative scheme was reinstated using Morel & Seddon's original coloured designs, surviving in the Royal Library. The black marble chimneypiece incorporating bronze figures of satyrs, originally supplied by B.L. Vulliamy for Carlton House in 1807, survived the fire unscathed but the splendid chandelier was less fortunate; most of its glass had to be renewed. The parquet floor designed by Ludwig Grüner in 1854 was damaged beyond repair in the fire and has been replaced. The walls are hung with portraits of George IV's siblings and the State Portraits of King George VI and Queen Elizabeth by Sir Gerald Kelly, painted at Windsor during the Second World War. Their fictive backgrounds were based on designs by Sir Edwin Lutyens.

CARVED TROPHIES

The doors incorporate superb carved and gilded limewood trophies from Carlton House. Those at the north end had to be recarved, and the others required extensive restoration.

Pictures

Sir William Beechey (1753–1839), *Princess Elizabeth*, 1795–7

Sir Gerald Kelly (1879–1972), *Queen Elizabeth, Consort of King George VI*, 1942–5

Sir William Beechey (1753–1839), *Princess Amelia*, 1795–7

Sir William Beechey (1753–1839), *Princess Sophia*, 1795–7

Sir Gerald Kelly (1879–1972), *King George VI*, 1942–5

Sir William Beechey (1753–1839), *Princess Mary*, 1795–7

Sir William Beechey (1753–1839), *Princess Augusta*, 1795–7

After John Hoppner, *George IV when Prince of Wales*, c.1800

John Hoppner (1758–1810), *Edward, Duke of Kent*, c.1800

Sir William Beechey (1753–1839), *Charlotte, Princess Royal*, c.1795

Furniture

Large suite of carved and giltwood seat furniture by Morel & Seddon, c.1828

Two rectangular sofa tables with inlaid amboyna tops and gilt-bronze mounts, by Morel & Seddon, c.1828

Two circular tables with gilt-bronze mounts, by Morel & Seddon, c.1829

Six tall French Empire gilt-bronze candelabra of antique form, by Pierre-Philippe Thomire. From the Throne Room and Old Throne Room at Carlton House

Pair of French Empire seven-light lazuli and gilt-bronze candelabra by Pierre-Philippe Thomire. Purchased by George IV, 1817

French Empire gilt-bronze clock representing the Spirit of the Arts and inscribed *Artium Genio*, by Pierre-Philippe Thomire. Bought by George IV, 1813

Pair of French ebony cabinets with gilt-bronze mounts and *pietra dura* panels, 1803. Acquired from M.-E. Lignereux for George IV by Sir Harry Featherstonhaugh

Pair of English ebony and *pietra dura* cabinets attributed to Robert Hume, c.1820. Purchased for George IV, 1825

Smaller pair of ebony, Boulle and *pietra dura* cabinets attributed to Robert Hume, c.1820. Purchased by George IV, 1825

An English carved and gilt beechwood pedestal supported by winged griffins, attributed to Tatham, Bailey & Saunders, c.1811

Large cut-glass and gilt-bronze 28-light chandelier, c.1810

Porcelain

Large Chinese dark-blue porcelain vase mounted as a tripod. The gilt-bronze mounts are attributed to Pierre-Philippe Thomire, c.1790

Pair of tall late 18th-century Sèvres porcelain vases with gilt-bronze mounts

Pair of tall dark-blue Sèvres porcelain covered vases (*vase bachelier*), c.1767-70

Sculpture

Bronze figure of Mars attributed to Sebastian Slodtz, early 18th century

Bronze figure of Julius Caesar by Nicolas Coustou, early 18th century

RIGHT: *Sir Gerald Kelly,* King George VI *(above) and* Queen Elizabeth *(below),* 1942—5

State Dining Room

Intended as George IV's private dining room, the State Dining Room has since been used for more official entertaining. Queen Victoria, a great believer in fresh air, insisted that all the windows were thrown open and that the fires remained unlit during meals, even in winter. Outside the windows above the North Terrace is a platform on which the Queen's band would play. Today Her Majesty The Queen entertains guests here for lunch during Ascot week and during the evening for 'dine and sleep' parties every Easter.

The Dining Room has twice been damaged by fire, in 1853 and 1992. The later fire completely consumed all the walls, floor and ceiling and not one decorative element remained. The two chief casualties of the fire were in this room: a large sideboard designed by Pugin, and Beechey's painting *George III at a Review*, both of which had been deemed too large to remove while the re-wiring project took place. The room has been restored to Wyatville's gothic design.

The rosewood furniture in this room was in part designed by the young A.W.N. Pugin, working for Morel & Seddon around 1827, when he was only 15 years old.

Pictures

George Knapton (1698–1778), *Family of Frederick, Prince of Wales*, 1751. The recently widowed Augusta, Princess of Wales, poses with her children in front of a portrait of the late Prince. The future George III is second from the left

Benjamin Constant (1845–1902), *Queen Victoria*, 1899

Furniture

Suite of gothic revival rosewood and partly gilt dining-room furniture with gilt-bronze mounts, by Morel & Seddon from designs by A.C. and A.W.N. Pugin, 1828. The large sideboard is a modern replica, by N.E.J. Stevenson, of the original destroyed in the 1992 fire

Gilt beechwood dining chairs originally supplied for Carlton House by Tatham & Bailey, 1815

Eight patinated bronze lamps by Vulliamy, 1811, on modern *scagliola* (imitation marble) pedestals

French mantel clock with Sèvres porcelain panels depicting the history of timekeeping. Presented to Queen Victoria by King Louis-Philippe at Windsor Castle in 1844

Pair of patinated bronze candelabra with figures of the infant Hercules and the serpent, by Vulliamy, *c.*1810

Metalwork

Large gilt-bronze table centrepiece perfume-burner with a statuette of the Egyptian bull god Apis, early 19th century. Purchased by George IV, 1811

Large gilt-bronze centrepiece perfume burner with patinated trumpeting figures, perhaps by P.-P. Thomire, late 18th century

Large gilt-bronze perfume burner centrepiece with female figures and winged horses, early 19th century

Two large hexagonal gilt-bronze candelabra. Purchased by George IV, 1811

Two gilt-bronze candelabra with griffin bases, early 19th century

Porcelain

Massive Russian porcelain vase with gilt-bronze handles and mounts, painted with views of the palaces of Peterhof and Tsarskoe Selo. Presented to Queen Victoria by Tsar Nicholas I, 1844 *(see right)*

Octagon Dining Room

This small dining room is used by members of The Queen's Household when the Court is in residence at Easter. It occupies Brunswick Tower, which was built at the north-east corner of the castle by Wyatville for picturesque effect. During the 1992 fire the internal floors collapsed and the tower acted as a flue through which flames shot 15 metres (50 feet) into the sky. Miraculously, the marble chimneypiece survived the intense heat. Analysis of the vitrified bricks showed that temperatures had approached 820° Centigrade.

China Corridor

This circulation corridor was added by Wyatville outside the medieval curtain wall. The display cases were originally intended for some of George IV's collection of arms and armour. The displays of porcelain, introduced by Queen Mary in the 1920s, include a large quantity of Chinese and Japanese porcelain of the seventeenth and early eighteenth centuries, and parts of several English and continental dining services.

Furniture
Set of gothic revival stools, made of oak and pollard oak by Morel & Seddon, 1827-8, from designs by A.W.N. Pugin

Three gothic revival oak side tables, veneered in pollard oak, by Morel & Seddon, c.1828

Set of gothic revival oak chairs, mid-19th century

Oak extending table by Johnstone, Norman & Co., 1891

Clock
French patinated and gilt-bronze mantel clock by Manière, with figures emblematic of Time and Study, early 19th century

Chandelier
Gilt-bronze gothic revival chandelier, the design attributed to A.W.N. Pugin, made by Hancock & Rixon, c.1828

MALACHITE URN

Presented to Queen Victoria by Tsar Nicholas I in 1839, this is one of the largest examples outside Russia. During the 1992 fire it filled up with hose water, causing the malachite veneers to fall off in many places, requiring a lengthy restoration.

Grand Reception Room

Of all the rooms created for George IV, the Grand Reception Room perhaps best epitomises his love of all things French. Intended as the principal ballroom of the castle, it is one of the earliest rococo revival interiors in England, starting a fashion that was to last throughout the nineteenth century. The walls incorporate eighteenth-century French panelling, extended in height by the addition of moulded stucco by Francis Bernasconi.

This was the site of Edward III's Great Staircase, at the heart of the medieval palace. The floor still incorporates fourteenth-century roof-timbers, reused during the seventeenth century when the room became the King's Guard Chamber. From here it was possible to enter the King's apartments to the west and St George's Hall and the chapel to the south. During the 1992 fire Bernasconi's plaster ceiling collapsed and the walls were badly burnt and water damaged. The three chandeliers, just reinstalled following complete restoration and rewiring, were extremely badly damaged, but were once again restored and reinstated. The room itself was entirely restored and all the gilding renewed. The original parquet floor survived the fire; blocks that were singed by the flames have been reversed.

Tapestries

Six episodes from the Story of Jason, woven at the Gobelins factory in Paris between 1776 and 1779, by Cozette and Audran, after paintings by Jean-François de Troy. Purchased in Paris for George IV, 1825

Jason pledges his faith to Medea, who promises to help him with her sorcery

Glauce, daughter of King Creon of Thebes, is killed by the magic robe presented to her by Medea

Jason puts the dragon to sleep, takes possession of the Golden Fleece and departs with Medea

Jason, unfaithful to Medea, marries Glauce

Soldiers sprung from the dragon's teeth turn their weapons against each other

Medea stabs her two sons by Jason, sets fire to Corinth and departs for Athens

Furniture

Pieces from two suites of upholstered giltwood seat furniture (some with gilt-metal enrichments) by Morel & Seddon, 1828, covered with late 18th-century Beauvais tapestry. The set was extended for King George V and Queen Mary in the 1920s

Pair of giltwood tables with marble tops and griffin supports by Tatham, Bailey & Sanders, 1814. Made for Carlton House

Pair of giltwood tables with marble tops and sphinx supports, mid-18th century and later

Two large circular tables by Morel & Seddon, with inlaid amboyna tops and winged-lion supports, c.1828

Chinoiserie gilt-bronze clock and matching thermometer with painted bronze figures of a peacock and a Chinese man and woman. Supplied by Vulliamy for Brighton Pavilion, 1819

Three massive English gilt-bronze and cut-glass chandeliers, c.1830

Aubusson flat woven floral carpet with the cipher of King George V

Pair of Chinese blue porcelain candelabra with 18th-century French gilt-bronze mounts

RIGHT: *Gilt and patinated bronze clock by Vulliamy, 1819.*

Two pairs of late 18th-century Chinese dark-blue porcelain vases, mounted as candelabra; the gilt-bronze chinoiserie mounts by Vulliamy, 1819. From the Royal Pavilion, Brighton

Pair of 18th-century Sèvres porcelain candelabra with gilt-bronze mounts

Garnitures of late 18th-century French marble vases with gilt-bronze mounts

Sculpture

Russian urn veneered with malachite. Presented to Queen Victoria by Tsar Nicholas I, 1839

Bronze group of Louis XV supported on a shield, cast from a model by Jean-Baptiste II Lemoyne (1704–78) for an unexecuted monument intended for the city of Rouen, 1776

Bronze bust of the Prince de Condé, after Jérome Derbais, early 18th century

Bronze bust of Marshal Turenne after Jérome Derbais, early 18th century

Bronze bust of Cardinal Richelieu, by Jean Warin, 17th century

Bronze bust of Charles I by Hubert Le Sueur, 17th century

Bronze centrepiece group of the Abduction of Persephone by Pluto in a chariot, French, 18th century

Bronze group of Hercules, Antaeus and Gaea, French, 18th century

Bronze group of Pluto and Persephone after Bernini, French, 18th century

Pair of bronze vases in the form of grotesque figures, French, 18th century

LEFT: Jason pledges his faith to Medea. *One of a set of six Gobelins tapestries, 1776–9.*

Garter Throne Room

In this room new Knights and Ladies of the Garter are invested with the insignia of the Order by The Queen. It was Queen Victoria's principal Throne Room, where she received important visitors seated on the magnificent Indian ivory throne.

Wyatville created the space by combining the former King's Presence Chamber with the eastern end of the King's Privy or Audience Chamber. The former division between the two rooms is marked by the shallow arch two-thirds of the way in. These two rooms originally lay at the beginning of the King's apartments. The seventeenth-century ceilings were replaced by Wyatville's ingenious design in plaster incorporating the insignia and collar of the Order of the Garter. The wainscot dado and cornice survive from the seventeenth century, but the oak wall panels were installed by Queen Mary in the 1920s. The limewood carvings by Grinling Gibbons and his assistants were reused from other rooms.

Pictures

Gainsborough Dupont (1754–97), *George III*, 1795

Studio of Sir Thomas Lawrence, *George IV*, c.1828

Sir Martin Archer Shee (1769–1850), *William IV*, 1833

Sir James Gunn (1893–1964), *Queen Elizabeth II* 1954–6

Franz Xaver Winterhalter (1806–73), *Prince Albert*, 1843

Franz Xaver Winterhalter (1806–73), *Queen Victoria*, 1843

Studio of Sir Godfrey Kneller, *George I*, c.1715

Sir Godfrey Kneller (1646–1723), *George II*, 1716

Furniture

Indian ivory chair of state and footstool. Presented to Queen Victoria in 1851 by the Maharajah of Travancore and shown at the Great Exhibition in the same year

Giltwood armchairs in the gothic style, designed by James Wyatt for the Palace of Westminster and made by John Russell and Charles Elliott, 1807

Three giltwood pier tables, early 19th century

English giltwood stools of three patterns, late 18th and early 19th centuries

ABOVE: Reception of the Ambassadors of Siam, November 1857, *watercolour by R.T. Landells.*

SIR JAMES GUNN, *QUEEN ELIZABETH II*, 1954–6

This is the official or State Portrait of Her Majesty The Queen. She wears her Coronation dress and robe of state, the George and collar of the Garter and George IV's Diamond Diadem. She carries the sceptre, and the Imperial State Crown rests on a table beside her.

Two English gilt gesso torchères, early 18th century

Giltwood throne canopy, late 18th-century with 19th-century velvet hangings

Giltwood throne chair, made by White, Allom & Co. for the Coronation, 1953

Three giltwood chandeliers, copied from an 18th-century original at Hampton Court, 20th century

Pair of Chinese blue porcelain vases with gilt decoration and French gilt-bronze mounts, mid-18th century. Purchased by Queen Mary in 1920

Sculpture
Three white marble and gilt-bronze mounted models of the ancient Roman arches of Titus, Constantine and Septimius Severus by Giovacchino and Pietro Belli, 1808-15. From the Library at Carlton House

ABOVE: Sunday morning in the Lower Ward, *watercolour by Joseph Nash, 1846.*

Quadrangle

On leaving the State Apartments, the visitor enters Engine Court. At the opposite corner of the Quadrangle is the Sovereign's Entrance, which gives access to the private apartments on the south and east sides. All along these sides is the Grand Corridor, added by Wyatville for George IV.

Having served as the tilt-yard in medieval and Tudor times, the Quadrangle still provides the setting for many colourful ceremonies. During state visits, the foreign head of state takes the salute here as the Guard of Honour marches past. When The Queen is in official residence, the Changing of the Guard takes place here.

The bronze equestrian statue of Charles II was cast in 1679 by Josias Ibach from a model by Grinling Gibbons. The statue, originally placed in the centre of the Quadrangle, was moved to its present position by Wyatville. The tall granite pedestal incorporates marble panels carved by Gibbons for the original limestone pedestal.

St George's Chapel

St George's Chapel lies on the north side of the Lower Ward. Work on the present chapel began under Edward IV in 1475 and the east end or Quire (choir) was completed by 1484 with a wooden roof. The magnificent stone fan vaulting seen by visitors today was added shortly afterwards, by Henry VII, when the nave was also finished. The chapel was finally completed under Henry VIII in 1528, with the fan vault over the crossing. The exterior of the chapel is faced in Taynton limestone from Oxfordshire.

The spiritual home of the Order of the Garter and the site of a number of royal tombs and memorials, the chapel also ranks as one of the finest examples of the Perpendicular style in the country. This style is characterised by large windows, tall, slender pillars and an overall impression of soaring grace and elegance. At least three services take place every day in the chapel, and visitors are welcome to attend.

LEFT: *Originally forming the western entrance to Henry III's chapel, this door, decorated with iron scrollwork fashioned around 1246, is at the east end of St George's Chapel.*

ABOVE: *Engraved brass stall plate of one of the Garter Knights.*

ABOVE: *Memorial by Matthew Wyatt to King George IV's daughter, Princess Charlotte, who died in childbirth in 1817.*

OPPOSITE: *The fan-vaulted ceiling of the Quire, with the banners of the Knights of the Garter.*

Features of note in the nave include the West Window, 11 metres (36 feet) high, and incorporating early sixteenth-century stained glass. The nave also includes four chantry chapels, founded so that perpetual prayers could be said for the souls of the patrons and their families. Royal memorials in the nave include those of King George V and Queen Mary, and the spectacular monument to Princess Charlotte, only child of George IV, who died in childbirth in 1817. King George VI, Queen Elizabeth (The Queen Mother) and Princess Margaret are interred in a memorial chapel off the north Quire aisle. This chapel may be viewed from the aisle. Further tombs and memorials seen from the Quire include those of Edward IV, Henry VI, and King Edward VII and Queen Alexandra. The entrance to the vault containing the coffins of Henry VIII and Charles I is under the centre of the Quire.

Visitors can also see some remarkable examples of medieval woodwork and ironwork. The west door of the original chapel (now the Albert Memorial Chapel) dating back to 1240 is preserved in the Ambulatory. The seats in the fifteenth-century Quire stalls tip up to reveal carved misericords. The magnificent Sovereign's Stall, used by The Queen today, was constructed in the late eighteenth century. The front row of seats at the west end is used by the men and boys of the choir, who sing at eight services per week.

The banners of the Knights of the Garter hang over their stalls in the Quire. There have been over nine hundred Knights since the foundation of the Order, and around 700 engraved and enamelled brass stall plates of former Knights are fastened to the backs of the stalls.

Treasures of the chapel to be seen on leaving the Quire include Edward III's 2-metre (6-foot) long sword, probably the weapon he wielded in battle, together with a likeness of the King painted in 1615. Close by is an unusual wooden font from the 1600s. These are in the south or 'pilgrimage' aisle of the chapel, where visitors can see an alms box, made around 1480 by John Tresilian to encourage pilgrims to the chapel to leave donations. As well as the tomb of Henry VI – renowned for his piety – pilgrims also came to see the Cross Gneth, a reliquary presented by Edward III and said to have included a portion of the True Cross, and the Schorne Chantry, named in honour of a Buckinghamshire priest who died in 1314 leaving a reputation as

Separate publications are available on the Albert Memorial Chapel and St George's Chapel

a great healer of the sick. The Cross Gneth is commemorated by a boss on the ceiling of the east end of the aisle. The actual Cross Gneth may have stood in one of two niches near the boss, but was probably destroyed during the Reformation.

It is usually possible for visitors to enter the Horseshoe Cloister, built around the west end of the chapel, where The Queen and the Knights of the Garter enter and leave the chapel on Garter Day.

Albert Memorial Chapel

The richly decorated interior of this fifteenth-century chapel, originally built as Henry III's chapel in the 1240s, was created by George Gilbert Scott for Queen Victoria to commemorate her husband Prince Albert.

It is possible for visitors to look inside at the vaulted ceiling, with a gold mosaic by Antonio Salviati, and the inlaid marble panels by Henri de Triqueti around the lower walls. The marble effigy of Prince Albert at the altar end is also by Triqueti.

The chapel is now dominated by the masterpiece of the sculptor and jeweller Alfred Gilbert, the tomb of the Duke of Clarence and Avondale, the elder son of King Edward VII, who died in 1892.

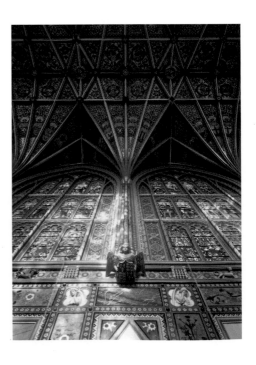

LEFT: *Figure of St George by Alfred Gilbert on the tomb of the Duke of Clarence.*

RIGHT: *The interior of the Albert Memorial Chapel.*